# Vocabulary
# Instruction
## *for Academic Success*

**Authors**

Hallie Kay Yopp, Ruth Helen Yopp, and Ashley Bishop

SHELL EDUCATION

# Vocabulary Instruction for Academic Success

**Editors**
Kristy Grabow, M.A.Ed.
Jodene Lynn Smith, M.A.

**Assistant Editor**
Leslie Huber, M.A.

**Editorial Director**
Lori Kamola, M.S.Ed.

**Editor-in-Chief**
Sharon Coan, M.S.Ed.

**Editorial Manager**
Gisela Lee, M.A.

**Creative Director/
Cover Design**
Lee Aucoin

**Print Production Manager/
Interior Layout Designer**
Don Tran

**Consultant**
Joan Irwin, M.A.

**Publisher**
Corinne Burton, M.A.Ed.

## Shell Education

5301 Oceanus Drive
Huntington Beach, CA 92649-1030

**http://www.shelleducation.com**

ISBN 978-1-4258-0266-0

© 2009 Shell Education

Made in U.S.A.

# Table of Contents

# Foreword

For many years we have known that vocabulary knowledge is a good predictor of academic success. We have also known that understanding the meanings of words in a passage is necessary for comprehension. It is surprising then that, until recently, not much attention was paid to vocabulary instruction in schools. Fortunately, more researchers and educators are now writing about the appropriate pedagogy for developing vocabulary knowledge. *Vocabulary Instruction for Academic Success* is a welcome addition to this topic.

Vocabulary knowledge can be thought of in many different ways: Is *knowing a word* the ability to provide a definition, use it in a sentence, recognize when it is being used inappropriately, know the connotations, know multiple meanings, know how to pronounce it, or all of the above? What is academic vocabulary? How does it differ from "everyday" vocabulary? How do we teach it effectively? Yopp, Yopp, and Bishop ask us to think about these issues and provide answers to these questions.

The authors give us a definition of academic vocabulary and stress the importance of emphasizing it in our classrooms. They argue that the words we choose and how we use them, help develop our students' vocabularies—why talk about *the main character* when we can talk about *the protagonist*? They also go beyond simply teaching academic vocabulary, and offer various perspectives about vocabulary development.

Experts agree that we cannot formally teach all of the words that students need to know. Students must learn many words from oral language and from wide reading in order to be academically successful. Yopp, Yopp, and Bishop place these two sources of vocabulary knowledge firmly at the forefront of the book. They provide information about how to structure classrooms to include discourse that will encourage word learning, and they include excellent ideas for developing independent and oral reading.

The authors held my attention throughout this book through practical teaching suggestions and examples of students' and teachers' work. The authors also demonstrate their familiarity with classrooms, teachers, and students by drawing from different grade levels and subject areas, and offering a wealth of information and ideas. They provide answers to questions that teachers often ask, such as "What words should I teach?" "Are there some suffixes that are more important to teach than others?" "How can I teach my students to use context effectively?"

I happen to love words—their richness and complexity; the way they sound; the way they feel on my tongue. One of my favorite words is "sassafras" because of its "mouth feel." Unfortunately many students do not feel this way, and it is one of our jobs as teachers to encourage a love of words. One way to do this is to develop word consciousness which is the subject of one of the chapters in *Vocabulary Instruction for Academic Success*. It talks about the importance of making students aware of words, and in doing so, providing opportunities for them to enjoy and revel in vocabulary. In this chapter, and throughout the book, the authors provide multiple ways to make this happen.

I direct a summer program for students with reading difficulties. When asked what they want to learn over the summer, many respond "more words." They know that word knowledge is a key to academic success. This book is a great resource for teachers to improve their vocabulary instruction so that all students can be confident in their word knowledge.

Peter J. Fisher
Professor, Reading and Language, National-Louis University
coauthor of *Teaching Vocabulary in All Classrooms*

# First Words

---

*"When I use a word," Humpty Dumpty said, in a rather scornful tone, "it means just what I choose it to mean, neither more nor less."*

*"The question is," said Alice, "whether you can make words mean so many different things."*

*"The question is," said Humpty Dumpty, "which is to be master—that's all."*

—Lewis Carroll

---

This is a text about vocabulary and the role it has in students' academic success. More importantly, *Vocabulary Instruction for Academic Success* focuses on the critical role teachers have in actively teaching vocabulary and vocabulary skills to today's students. Our first words are about two teachers and their impact on one student.

**Teacher 1/Kindergarten:** When Chad was four, during the summer before he began kindergarten, he and his dad made frequent trips to the library. At this early age, Chad already had favorite authors, his absolute favorite being Mercer Mayer. When his father asked him why he enjoyed Mayer's books so much, Chad stated, "I like his pictures and the words he uses." Imagine Chad's disappointment when on one library visit, he found a visit, he found a Mayer book about one of his favorite topics, frogs, only to discover the book had no written story. Mayer's wonderful illustrations were there, but the author had not written a single word.

Chad's dad had a solution. They would purchase their own copy of *A Boy, a Dog, and a Frog* (Mayer 1967), and Chad would be the author. Chad thought this was a fine idea. After they looked through the book, they went back and examined each page. As they did so, Chad told the story and Chad's dad wrote down, right below each illustration, the great words Chad used. When they were done, Chad's dad wrote, right on the cover, "Story by Chad Bishop."

Chad's kindergarten year began and, in no time at all, Teacher 1 presented her students with their first show-and-tell responsibility. They were to bring to class something that was especially important to them and share it with the class. Chad's choice was *A Boy, a Dog, and a Frog*, the book he had authored as summer came to an end. Chad, both nervous and proud, shared his book.

It was at this point that Teacher 1 did something that to this day, 30 years later, Chad has not forgotten. What did Teacher 1 do? She said to him, "Chad, what a great story and what grand words you used to tell it. You are quite an author. May I take your book home and show it to my husband?"

That afternoon, Chad came home with his chest out and head high. He was an author who used "grand" words and his teacher was showing his book to her husband! Chad has since earned his graduate degree in creative writing, completed two novels, and teaches high school English. There is little doubt that Teacher 1 had a significant impact on the professional role Chad assumed in life.

**Teacher 2/Late High School:** Chad, now well into his high school years, was on the varsity swim team, dating a foreign exchange student from Sweden, and writing for the school newspaper. He was also a conscientious student. The Friday before his first formal dance—he had asked the Swedish foreign exchange student, Eva, and she had accepted—his biology teacher assigned 200 vocabulary words to be defined, and the definitions were to be turned in the following Monday.

Chad did not greet the assignment with enthusiasm. He hadn't picked up his tux, his car was a mess, he needed a haircut, and the swim team had an important meet. Sunday was not an option, as he had to head down the road with his family to celebrate a grandparent's birthday. The family rallied. Chad's mom picked up the tux, his sister washed his car, and his dad provided transportation to the swim meet. During and even after the meet, while Eva and the dance beckoned, Chad searched for the definitions to 200 biology terms. He finished, donned his tux and, looking exceptionally handsome, raced out the door for an "Enchanted Evening Under the Sea." His mom, dad, and sister breathed a sigh of relief and ordered pizza.

On the way to the birthday celebration the next day, Chad thanked his parents, both of whom are teachers, and his sister. He stated, rather empathically, that if he ever teaches, he will never give his students an assignment like the one he was given. He wondered aloud how many of those definitions he would remember in 10 years, or even 10 days!

On Monday, because so few students had completed the definitions, the teacher rescinded the assignment. Chad was not happy and asked whether those who had completed the assignment should receive extra credit. The teacher complied. Although the extra credit made this experience a bit more tolerable, it could not buy back the hours he and his family lost that weekend because of a meaningless assignment.

These stories depict two teachers—one who had a tremendously positive impact and another who, unintentionally, had a rather negative impact.

As you read *Vocabulary Instruction for Academic Success*, you will see that current researchers make it very clear that vocabulary growth is essential to academic success and that the teacher's role in this growth is critical. You will also be provided with an abundance of vocabulary strategies—unlike the one used by Chad's high school teacher—that lead students to make new words their own, words they will then be able to use to enhance their social, academic, and professional worlds. Every chapter begins with an opening activity to help you start thinking about what is in the chapter ahead. Take the time to complete these short activities and even jot down your answers. At the end of each chapter, you may wish to revisit the chapter opener and see if any of your responses have changed. Each chapter concludes with a section called "Think About It." This is your opportunity to reflect on what you have learned in the chapter and to apply your learning. You are encouraged to turn to the chapter of this book that most appeals to you at this moment but hopefully you will visit the other chapters as well. Together, they provide you with important information that will support you as you develop a rich vocabulary program for your students. Best wishes.

# Chapter 1

# Vocabulary Instruction

## True or False?

Read the following statements and indicate whether you think each is true or false.

_____ 1. Students' vocabulary knowledge relates strongly to their reading comprehension.

_____ 2. Students' vocabulary knowledge relates strongly to their overall academic success.

_____ 3. As word recognition becomes less resource demanding, more general language skills such as vocabulary become the limiting factors on reading ability.

_____ 4. Inadequate vocabulary knowledge is a major factor in a child's failure in school.

_____ 5. Vocabulary knowledge in kindergarten and first grade is a significant predictor of reading comprehension in the middle and secondary grades.

_____ 6. Teaching vocabulary can improve reading comprehension.

*"The limits of my language are the limits of my mind. All I know is what I have words for."*

—Ludwig Wittgenstein

On a recent Monday afternoon, Eddie's father took him to the Department of Motor Vehicles to take his permit test. Fifteen-year-old Eddie had told his friends at school that it was his big day and that the next time they saw him, he would have his learner's permit. After completing the appropriate paperwork, Eddie was sent to the exam room and handed the test. He read and answered the questions carefully and submitted the test for scoring. Phew! He passed! Barely, but he passed. Eddie earned a score of 83 percent. One more wrong answer and he would have dipped below the cutoff of 80 percent. In the parking lot, Eddie's father reviewed the incorrect answers with Eddie and expressed confusion about his response to number 2. The question asked what drivers should do if a peace officer signals them to drive through a red light. Eddie's answer was to wait for a green light. When asked why he had not said to follow the police officer's directions, Eddie looked startled and said, "Oh! Is that what a peace officer is? A police officer? I didn't know that!" As soon as he understood the term *peace officer*, he knew the answer to the question. Of course you follow the police officer's directions!

Eddie's experience with his driving test illustrates how important words are to understanding and to success. Imagine if this question had been the one to tip the balance on Eddie's test, resulting in failure. What would the consequences have been? Eddie would not have been awarded his permit and therefore would not be allowed to drive. He would have had to wait a certain period of time before retaking the test. He would have had to tell his friends that he did not pass the test, and he might have felt embarrassed to admit this. He might have felt bad about himself. Instead, Eddie walked away proud and confident, and text messaged his friends the good news before he even left the premises. Word knowledge is important!

## The Importance of Vocabulary

Educators and educational researchers have known for years that vocabulary knowledge plays a significant role in reading comprehension. We saw that Eddie did not comprehend one of the test questions solely because he did not know one of the terms. Knowledge of words is essential to understanding text. Look at the brief passages below. Drawn from a variety of books ranging from those written for the very young to those written for adults, these examples reveal how important knowledge of words is to understanding text.

> "*On his way to town one day, the miller encountered the king.*" (Rumpelstiltskin, *adapted by Paul O. Zelinsky, no page given*)
>
> "*In the midst of this reverie, I heard a car pull into the driveway.*" (Bunnicula *by Deborah and James Howe, p. 4*)
>
> "*She wore her clothes so tight (hoping to look ethereal), she looked apoplectic.*" (Johnny Tremain *by Esther Forbes, p. 14*)
>
> "*Autumn was blithely indifferent to the tumult in the land that year.*" (Across Five Aprils *by Irene Hunt, p. 42*)
>
> "*At first Ekwefi accepted her, as she had accepted others—with listless resignation.*" (Things Fall Apart *by Chinua Achebe, p. 79*)

> *"His gentleness was never tinged by dogmatism; and his instructions were given with an air of frankness and good nature that banished every idea of pedantry."* (Frankenstein *by Mary Shelley, p. 29)*

Each of these examples demonstrates that the reader must have a vocabulary rich enough to support understanding of the text. What is a *miller*, and what does it mean to *encounter* a king? What is a *reverie*? What does it mean to look *ethereal* or *apoplectic*? What is *blithe indifference*, and what does *tumult* mean? What is *listless resignation*? And what do many of the words in the final example mean? Reading involves making sense of written language. In order to read successfully, we need to understand the words the author has chosen to use. The less we understand the individual words, the less we are able to comprehend the passage.

A large body of research confirms that vocabulary knowledge is positively related to a student's ability to comprehend text (Lehr, Osborn, and Hiebert 2004), and as the difficulty of words in a text increases, understanding of the text decreases. Although much remains to be learned, the relationship between word knowledge and comprehension is unequivocal. Further, there is evidence that instruction in vocabulary positively affects comprehension (Baumann, Kame'enui, and Ash 2003).

Vocabulary knowledge is clearly crucial for success in reading. Look at Eddie! However, its influence does not stop with reading. Vocabulary knowledge also plays a significant role in overall academic success (Lehr et al. 2004). For instance, notice the importance of understanding words in this hint provided in class one day by a Spanish teacher to his English-speaking students:

> *"The meaning of the Spanish word* detestar *is easy to remember because it is related to the English word* detest.*"*

A student who does not know what *detest* means finds this hint useless. He cannot take advantage of the teacher's comment (in fact, he may be frustrated by it) and thus must work harder than some of his peers to learn the Spanish word. If the teacher shares many of these types of hints, then the students with limited vocabularies are likely to be less efficient in learning the new content than their peers.

Here is another example of vocabulary's impact on academic achievement: Think about a third-grade student's prospect for successful learning when he or she does not know the words *decomposer* and *fungus*, and the teacher, addressing grade-level life science content, says the following:

"*Decomposers recycle matter. A good example of a decomposer is fungus.*"

Also think about how a narrow understanding of the word *recycle* might lead to misunderstanding the term as used in this context.

Students' knowledge of words impacts their achievement in all areas of the curriculum because words are necessary for communicating the content. As classroom teachers know, students have difficulty understanding and expressing the concepts and principles of the content areas if they do not know the specialized vocabulary that represents those concepts and principles. It is nearly impossible for students to read about, talk about, write about, and understand information about volcanoes, for example, if they do not know the words *magma*, *lava*, *vent*, and *erupt*. Indeed, educational authorities advise us that "wide vocabulary and broad knowledge go together" (Hirsch 2003) and that "vocabulary knowledge *is* knowledge" (Stahl 2005).

The language demands of academic learning are significant. The richer the students' *academic language*, the more likely they will experience success with the content. Academic language is defined as "the language that is used by teachers and students for the purpose of acquiring new knowledge and skills … imparting new information, describing abstract ideas, and developing students' conceptual understanding" (Chamot and O'Malley 2007, as cited in Bailey 2007). Simply put, academic language is the language of schools and can be contrasted with everyday informal speech. Bailey identifies three features of academic language: lexical, grammatical, and discourse. *Lexical* refers to vocabulary and includes both general academic terms such as *analyze, infer*, and *conclusion*, and specialized terms such as *evaporate, civilization*, and *perimeter*. *Grammatical* refers to sentence structures, and *discourse* refers to larger organizational features of language. Although the focus of this book is the lexical level—words—you will find that many of the strategies we share stimulate language interactions that support the acquisition of the grammatical and discourse features of academic language as well.

Vocabulary knowledge impacts reading and academic success, and—as we saw in the case of Eddie—it is significant in our daily lives and can have practical as well as social and emotional consequences. Vocabulary is positively related to higher-status occupations (Marzano 2004), communicates to the world what we know, and contributes to people's judgments about how smart we are (Stahl 2005). Individuals who can express themselves precisely and with appropriate language are more likely to make a positive impression on their employers, colleagues, and clients. Vocabulary enables us to communicate our needs, increasing the likelihood that we get them met, and it enables us to understand the needs of others.

For good reason, then, vocabulary development is currently receiving considerable attention in professional literature. Indeed, it was the subject of an extensive study by the National Reading Panel (NICHD 2000), has been the focus of numerous books published in the past decade, is a popular topic of presentations at national and state educational conferences, and was recently identified as "hot" on the International Reading Association's list of what's hot and what's not in literacy (Cassidy and Cassidy 2008).

Unfortunately, there is evidence that vast differences exist in the vocabularies of children—even before they enter schools. Hart and Risley (2003), for example, found that some children had far more exposure to words, far larger vocabularies, and faster rates of word acquisition than others. The researchers described an ever-widening gap among children and estimated that by age three, there was a 30-million-word difference in terms of number of words heard by children. Of great concern is that the rate of vocabulary growth measured at age three predicted performance on tests of vocabulary and language development at ages nine and ten among these children. Additionally, vocabulary use at age three was strongly associated with reading comprehension scores at ages nine and ten. White, Graves, and Slater (1990) also found large gaps among children, with some children learning an estimated 1,000 words per year between the first and fifth grades and others learning 5,000 words per year.

The large gap in vocabulary knowledge among students and the finding that these differences are highly related to future performance in reading, in schooling, and in life are alarming. Yet, as Beck, McKeown, and Kucan pointed out, historically there has not been much vocabulary instruction in schools—and this may be good news. Why good news? Because, as Beck et al. stated, "Perhaps it is not so much the case that those differences cannot be changed, but rather that little has been done to focus on making them change" (2000, 2). Thus, a concerted effort by teachers to provide a comprehensive vocabulary program may be what it takes to significantly impact students' vocabulary development and narrow the language gap. Research does, in fact, indicate that instruction makes a difference.

# What Teachers Should Know About Words and Word Learning

In this section, we share three fundamental understandings about words and word learning that we believe every teacher should know. The first is that word knowledge is complex. The second is that vocabulary instruction must be multifaceted. The third is that vocabulary instruction must be a curriculum-wide commitment.

## Word knowledge is complex.

To know a word is not simply to know its definition. Nagy and others (Nagy 2006; Nagy and Scott 2000) describe multiple dimensions of word knowledge, including knowledge of the word's phonological structure (i.e., What does it sound like?) and orthographic structure (i.e., How it is spelled?). For example, you may understand the word *solder* when you hear someone describe the process of joining two metallic pieces with a melted metal alloy, but do you recognize the word in print? If you saw the word in a list, would you be able to pronounce it (/sod/-/er/) and elicit its meaning? Or would you think it was a misprint of the word *soldier*? Word knowledge also includes information about the grammatical function of the word (i.e., How is it used in a sentence?) and its collocational behavior (i.e., What words usually appear with it?), as well as its stylistic uses. A student who is able to define a word is not necessarily also able to say the word, write the word, use the word in a sentence, and understand its connotative and metaphorical uses. In other words, there is much to know about words, and "knowing" them is not an all-or-none phenomenon.

In addition to being multidimensional, words often have multiple meanings, and the appropriate meaning for a word depends on the context in which it is used. The word *value*, for example, means something different in economics, mathematics, and art. Consider the use of the word *flat* in each of these sentences:

You are welcome to stay in my *flat* when you visit London.

I need a *flat* table to work on my project.

The trumpeter's notes were *flat*.

Her girlfriends admired her new *flats*.

I am *flat* broke.

A student who only knows one meaning of the word *flat* will be confused when he or she encounters the word in an unexpected context.

We share below more polysemous words. (Polysemous—/pol/-/e/-/se/-/məs/, used as an adjective to describe words that have more than one meaning; *poly* is of Greek origin and means "many.") Do you know more than one meaning for each of these words?

| | | |
|---|---|---|
| *acute* | *function* | *score* |
| *bank* | *attraction* | *bridge* |
| *difference* | *balance* | *produce* |
| *factor* | *mole* | *fret* |
| *foot* | *plate* | *tense* |

A substantial number of words in the English language are polysemous. In fact, Nagy (2006) observed that polysemous words are the rule rather than the exception, and Bailey (2007) noted that 60 to 70 percent of English words have multiple meanings. This feature of our language adds to the complexity of word knowledge and can be especially problematic for English language learners who may know the more common use of a word but lack understanding of its usage in less common or content-specific contexts.

Words are also heterogeneous; they are different. They differ in terms of their frequency of use, conceptual difficulty, level of abstractness, part of speech, role in text, and relationship to the content and the instructional goals. These differences dictate whether and how the words should be taught.

Adding to the complexity of words is the fact that they are interrelated. It is difficult to understand the meaning of *perpendicular* without understanding *right angle*, and understanding *bland* and *tasty* support an understanding of the word *delicious*.

What are the implications of word complexity for teachers? One major implication is that word learning occurs incrementally. A single exposure to a word generally does not result in rich understanding of the word. Encountering it in multiple and varied contexts is necessary for deep knowledge. Teachers must, therefore, provide numerous opportunities for students to interact with words in many contexts.

## Vocabulary instruction must be multifaceted.

Traditional vocabulary instruction involves asking students to learn the definitions of words, often by looking them up in the dictionary and recording them on paper. Remember Chad's high school biology teacher (in the "Introduction: First Words" section)? Based on what we know about the complexity of words and how words are learned, current thinking emphasizes a four-pronged approach to vocabulary instruction: providing extensive experiences with language, fostering word consciousness, teaching individual words, and teaching word-learning strategies.

- **Providing Extensive Experiences with Language**

  Language learning cannot occur without exposure to language. Research shows that most vocabulary is not directly taught; huge numbers of words are learned incidentally—through experiences with language. Thus, it is crucial that teachers establish language-rich environments.

This means that teachers must offer myriad opportunities for students to hear and engage with spoken language and to read, write, and engage with written language in multiple contexts. Indeed, Johnson (2001, 19) stated that "the best way to help schoolchildren expand their vocabularies ... is to provide plentiful, interactive oral language experiences throughout the elementary and middle grades." Nagy agreed that "experiences with rich oral language are critical for vocabulary growth" and noted that wide reading "is the primary engine that drives vocabulary growth" (2005, 29). Thus, one essential aspect of vocabulary instruction is exposure to plentiful language in the classroom.

- **Establishing a Word-Conscious Environment**

A second important component of vocabulary instruction is the promotion of students' interest in words and word learning. *Word consciousness* is the term used in literature to describe an awareness of and interest in words, and it involves both a cognitive and affective stance toward words. Students who are word-conscious think about and care about words and gain satisfaction and enjoyment from using them well (Graves and Watts-Taffe 2002). They are motivated to learn new words, and they seek out opportunities to experiment with words. Teachers can establish word-conscious environments by modeling and stimulating a curiosity about and enthusiasm for words. They can spark students' interest in words by exploring the etymology (history) and evolution of words. They can engage their students in word play and involve them in conducting investigations about words. When they promote word consciousness, teachers ensure their students' sustained vocabulary growth (Scott and Nagy 2004).

- **Teaching Words**

In addition to providing rich exposure to words and establishing a word-conscious environment, teachers should provide direct instruction of some word meanings. It is more efficient to teach the words students need to know for particular purposes than to wait for the words to be learned through context. In our example of words related to the study of volcanoes, for example, it is beneficial for the teacher to teach students the meanings of the words *magma*, *lava*, *vent*, and *erupt* rather than hope that the children come to understand the words through oral or written encounters. In any content area, there are words that are critical to understanding the topic under study. These words are known as *specialized content vocabulary*. They should be identified and taught. Similarly, when sharing a story with students, teachers should identify and teach words that are important to understanding the literature.

Research has revealed a number of principles that should guide teachers' efforts to effectively teach word meanings. They are the following:

- ✓ Instruction should provide more than definitional information about words. It must acknowledge the complexity of words and ensure that students are given ample contextual information about words (Stahl 1999; Tannenbaum, Torgesen, and Wagner 2006).

- ✓ Instruction should provide repeated exposure to words under study and multiple opportunities for students to use and practice the words (Blachowicz et al. 2006; NICHD 2000).

- ✓ Instruction should encourage students to think about relationships among word meanings (Blachowicz et al. 2006; NICHD 2000).

- ✓ Instruction should actively engage students in learning tasks (Beck et al. 2002; Kamil and Hiebert 2005; NICHD 2000).

- ✓ A variety of instructional practices should be employed (NICHD 2000).

- **Teaching Word-Learning Strategies**

  An effective vocabulary program is incomplete if teachers do not develop students' word-learning strategies. One strategy that supports students' abilities to continue to acquire new words is the use of word parts to unlock meaning. Acquiring an understanding of the meaning of frequently used prefixes, roots, and suffixes will support students' abilities to induce word meanings. For example, if students know that *uni-* means "one," they should be able to conclude that a *unicycle* is a one-wheeled cycle. Similarly, understanding the prefix *uni-* will contribute to students' understanding of *unify, unilateral, unidirectional, unicellular*, and *uniform*.

  A second word-learning strategy is the use of context. Students can be taught that sometimes text provides enough information to support understanding of an unknown word. For example, the use of the word *instead* in the following sentence signals to students that a contrast is being made between *abating* and *worsened*: Instead of abating, the storm worsened. Students who do not know the word *abating* can be taught to use the context to infer that it means "lessening."

  A third word-learning strategy is the effective use of a dictionary. The dictionary can be a powerful tool, especially when students are motivated to understand the meaning of a word.

## Vocabulary instruction must be a curriculum-wide commitment.

If students need to be provided with extensive language experiences, create word-conscious classrooms, and teach words and word-learning strategies, then vocabulary instruction cannot be relegated to a brief period of the day. It must permeate the day and extend through all areas of the curriculum. In order to ensure that students have opportunities to talk and read throughout the day, teachers need to highlight words in every subject matter and teach words and word-learning strategies in many contexts. Language must be addressed in every subject we teach. As Heritage, Silva, and Pierce (2007, 183) asserted, "All teachers need to be both content teachers and language teachers."

Vocabulary instruction is an obvious fit in our language arts programs. It is also a natural fit in the content areas because words are so important to learning subject matter. Words are expressions of concepts. We use the word *habitat*, for instance, to express the idea of a natural environment that provides food, shelter, water, and space for particular organisms. A *riparian habitat* is a particular type of habitat: a natural environment next to or affected by a water source such as a river that provides food, shelter, water, and space for particular organisms. The word *diameter* refers to the distance of a straight line that has endpoints on a circle's circumference and passes through the center point of a circle. (Notice how helpful it is to understand the terms *circumference* and *endpoints* when learning the word *diameter*.) Our understanding of these terms continues to be elaborated on and refined as we learn more about the content. As Hirsch (2003, 28) argued, "A coherent and extended curriculum is the most effective vocabulary builder."

Not only do the content areas provide rich, purposeful exposure to words in meaningful contexts, they also provide repeated exposure to words. Students hear the words used by their teachers and peers, they read the words in accompanying texts, they use the words as they discuss the content, and they incorporate the words into their own writing and presentations. The content areas can offer many opportunities to use new words, thus developing students' content vocabularies. As students explore a topic in depth, they are exposed to key vocabulary again and again.

# A Few Words About English Language Learners

Like all learners, English language learners need teachers who have a strong knowledge base and commitment to developing students' language. It is crucial that teachers work carefully to develop English language learners' academic vocabularies. Each of the strategies we suggest in this book can be used effectively with English language learners. In addition, we want to remind teachers of the following important principles for supporting English language learners as they develop their vocabularies in a new language:

- Encourage native language development. It is easier for individuals to learn new labels for already-known concepts than to learn new concepts. For instance, the word *indifferent* is easier to learn in a new language if students already know the concept and its verbal representation in their native languages.

- Create a safe, comfortable, and nonthreatening atmosphere that encourages students to use their new language and ensure that they have authentic reasons to engage in language use with you and one another.

- Respect and draw on students' backgrounds and experiences and build connections between the known and the new.

- Know your students and capitalize on their interests. All of us are more likely to attend to and communicate about what we find fascinating.

- Model and scaffold language use.

- Take advantage of the cognates that exist between languages. For instance, many English and Spanish words, such as *family* and *familia*, have a common origin.

- Make use of realia, concrete materials, visuals, pantomime, and other nonlinguistic representations of concepts to make input comprehensible. Write new words on the board as they are shared or provide each student with a set of cards that contain the words. That way students can see the words as well as hear them.

- Introduce new words in rich contexts that support meaning.

- Ensure that students have ample opportunities for social interactions, especially in the context of content learning. English language learners need many occasions to practice the academic language they are learning.

- Provide wait time. Allowing students time to put their thoughts into words is important for all students, but it is especially so for students who are learning to communicate in a new language.

- Keep your expectations high for all students—and for yourself as their teacher. Work for depth and breadth of understanding of challenging content and promote critical thinking.

# Conclusion

The primary purposes of this chapter are to convince you that vocabulary instruction is important and to provide you with the big picture of how to support vocabulary development in your classroom. Now explore the suggestions and strategies provided for enhancing your students' word knowledge. Chapter 2 shares numerous suggestions for providing students with rich oral language experiences. Chapter 3 presents information about the incidental word learning that occurs through exposure to text—as students engage in wide reading on their own and as they listen to books that are read aloud. Chapter 4 provides ideas for promoting an enthusiasm for words through a word-conscious classroom. Chapter 5 offers a wealth of suggestions for teaching individual words, and Chapter 6 describes independent word-learning strategies.

If you read this chapter from beginning to end, you may have by now forgotten the quiz that opened this chapter. Now would be a good time to revisit the statements. Do you have new insights? Have your answers changed? Although you may have been surprised as you began reading this chapter to learn that all six statements are true, we suspect that at this point, you are not surprised. Word learning is important, the consequences of not knowing words can be long-lasting and profound, and teachers can make a difference in students' vocabulary development.

# Think About It!

Read the brief scenario below and identify at least four ways that Mrs. Sanchez promoted the vocabulary development of her third-grade students.

Mrs. Sanchez greeted her students with a cheerful "Salutations!" as they bustled into the classroom on a chilly Wednesday morning. The children looked at her quizzically, so after they settled into their desks, she explained that *salutations* is another word for "greetings" and is often used to say "hello and welcome" when you see someone. She said she likes the sound of the word as it rolls off her tongue and invited the students to say the word with her—"Salutations!"—and then to turn and greet each other with the word. She wrote it on the board and encouraged the students to use the word when they see their friends on the playground at recess and lunch. As she began her morning routine, she asked the students to turn to their neighbors and review yesterday's science lesson by "expressing in sequential order" the steps of the experiment they conducted.

Mrs. Sanchez engaged in several vocabulary-building strategies in the first few minutes of her school day. Did you identify the following?

1. She expressed an interest in words, thus promoting word consciousness.

2. She used words that stretched the students' vocabularies (e.g., *salutations, expressing, sequential*) thus creating a language-rich environment.

3. She provided an explanation of *salutations*, including when and how it is used, thus teaching a new word.

4. She asked the students to use the word now and at recess and lunchtime, thus encouraging students to apply the word in other settings.

5. She provided the students with an oral language experience focused on academic learning, thus creating a language-rich environment.

6. In addition, it is clear from this brief scenario that Mrs. Sanchez's curriculum includes science. Students learn new words as they learn new content, and Mrs. Sanchez's content-area instruction will contribute to her students' world knowledge and word knowledge.

# Promoting Oral Language

## Possible Sentences

Read and think about each set of words or terms below. Do you know what the words mean? Have you seen or heard them before? How do they fit together? Write a sentence for each set of words, making sure to use all four words in the sentence. You might need to guess what some words mean in order to include them in your sentence.

**Set 1:** hothouse    opportunity    linguistic input    vocabulary

Sentence: _____

_____

_____

_____

_____

**Set 2:** output    I-R-E    expressive    language

Sentence: _____

_____

_____

_____

_____

*"Language ... is the grandest triumph of the human intellect."*

—Walt Whitman

Opportunities to hear rich language and to use language in many settings are crucial for vocabulary development. Teachers must create classrooms that are *linguistic hothouses*—ones that nourish language by deliberately exposing students to high-quality, cognitively challenging verbal input across the curriculum and by intentionally stimulating students' active use of language in diverse contexts. In this chapter, we discuss the importance of surrounding students with many models of complex language and ensuring that all students have many opportunities to use language themselves. Finally, we share strategies that stimulate oral language interactions.

## Language Input

Students must have many opportunities to hear rich language. They must be provided with an environment in which there are models of precise and sophisticated vocabulary. You may recall from Chapter 1 that there are striking differences in the oral vocabularies of children as young as three. What we want to point out here is that research reveals that these differences can be largely accounted for by the language in the children's environment (Hart and Risley 1995). It probably will not surprise you to learn that the more words children hear and the greater variety of words they hear, the more words and greater variety of words they use. Likewise, students in classrooms with teachers who use syntactically-complex speech demonstrate more syntactically-complex speech at the end of the year than their counterparts in other classrooms (Huttenlocher et al. 2002). Language development does not happen without exposure, that is, without input. Four key sources of language input in the classroom are the teacher, the students, the text, and the curriculum.

## The Teacher

We learn language through interactions with others who have more skills than ourselves. In the classroom, the more skilled language user is you, the teacher. Teachers are models of language when they make announcements, give directions, teach lessons, respond to questions, work with small groups, and engage in conversations with individuals. Every utterance is an opportunity to expand students' language. Teachers who are conscious of their word choices during each of these interactions and who intentionally use a rich vocabulary offer a fertile setting for students to develop their vocabularies.

We don't often think about the words we use, yet if we hope to support students' vocabulary development, we must be mindful of our word choices. We need to raise our consciousness about the precision of our language. Notice the teachers' word choices in the scenarios below.

- Mr. Watkins, a junior high school science teacher, moved through a room full of students engaged in a laboratory investigation. Stopping at one group's table, he listened to their conversation about pouring a liquid from one container to another. He pointed to each container and reminded the students that one type is called a *flask* and the other is called a *beaker*. He was deliberate in his use of the words and was pleased when he later read the group's written report of the investigation, noting that they had used the precise terminology.

- A third-grade classroom teacher guided her students to fold a piece of paper as they worked on a project. Rather than saying, "Fold the paper hot-dog style," Ms. Lan demonstrated to students how to hold their papers, then asked them to make a *horizontal* fold.

- Mrs. McMann complimented her kindergarteners, telling them she was pleased with how *conscientious* they were about cleaning the classroom after a messy activity. She continued by rephrasing her sentiments, indicating that she was delighted they were thorough, thoughtful, and careful in their efforts; they took the task of cleaning up seriously!

- A second-grade student was conversing with her teacher about a weekend soccer game during which the student had scored a goal. The enthusiastic student told Mrs. Kafka that for weeks she had been practicing kicking the ball at home. The teacher responded, "You must have found scoring a goal very *gratifying*! In other words, you were probably very pleased and satisfied to know your practice paid off! Good for you!"

- Sixth-grade teacher Miss Nguyen told her students she felt *ambivalent* about whether the class should accept another class's invitation to participate in an upcoming field trip. She then explained the pros and cons, from her perspective, of joining the other class.

- "I am *nonplussed*, completely perplexed, by your behavior," Mr. Archel told his normally responsive students one afternoon when they disregarded his requests to settle down.

These teachers were thoughtful in their use of rich vocabulary as they interacted with students. Aware of their influence as language models, they intentionally used words that would stretch their students' vocabularies, while providing ample support (e.g., through pointing to objects, modeling, and rephrasing) so that students understood. Unfortunately, there are many missed opportunities for vocabulary development in classrooms, as in these observations:

- A preschool teacher gestured and repeatedly told a student to bring her "that thing." "Get me that thing, Johnny. No, that thing. Over there. Hand me that thing, please." The child kept looking around until he finally realized what the teacher was referring to: a tambourine.

- A sixth-grade teacher ignored the morning announcement in which the principal noted that the school's Word of the Week was *assiduous* and encouraged all students to demonstrate that quality. At the conclusion of the principal's announcements, Ms. Devereaux, who had been preoccupied with shuffling through papers on her desk, promptly asked her students to prepare for the spelling pretest.

- Ms. Wilson did not respond to her fourth-grade students' quizzical expressions and mumbles of "What did he do?" when the custodian, walking through the classroom, commented that he had *replenished* the paper towel dispenser during recess. She gave him a quick nod of thanks and directed the students' attention to the math problems she had written on the board.

- Introducing a new novel, Mr. Gallen indicated to his tenth graders that the main character is a brave leader. (Why not say that the *protagonist* is an *intrepid* leader? The students likely learned the terms *main character* and *brave* in early elementary school.)

We do not learn words to which we have never been exposed. The reason you don't speak Malagasy (assuming you don't) is that you aren't surrounded by Malagasy (the language spoken in Madagascar); you don't hear it, and you don't see it in print. Likewise, a child who is never exposed to the word *tambourine* will not learn the word. Words we never come into contact with cannot become a part of our lexicon.

Interestingly, research demonstrates that we can learn words from conversations in which we ourselves are not direct participants. Simply being in an environment where we hear others use rich vocabulary contributes to our vocabulary growth; even as bystanders, we learn (Akhtar, Jipson, and Callanan 2001).

Teachers who attend to vocabulary development not only purposefully use rich language, they also draw students' attention to the terminology they are using. "I'm going to use a word you may not know," they say. Or, "Did you notice that word?"

As one of the most influential sources of language input in the classroom, teachers must do the following:

- **Deliberately plan to use rich language in their interactions with students**. Mr. Watkins, the junior high science teacher who used the words *flask* and *beaker*, purposefully considered ahead of time what language would be useful for his students to own. Ms. Lan, too, planned to use the word *horizontal* when demonstrating to her second graders how to fold their papers. Their language use was intentional.

- **Remain alert for informal opportunities to use rich language**. Mrs. McMann, Mrs. Kafka, and Miss Nguyen used sophisticated language when responding to their students' actions and personal narratives. They listened to their students, displayed a genuine interest in what they had to say, and seized the opportunity to expose their students to new terminology in the course of authentic communicative interactions.

- **Intentionally draw attention to interesting words**. When the custodian used the word *replenished*, Ms. Wilson could have commented to her class on his word use, defining the term and asking her students to think about things they have replenished recently. Does anyone replenish the salt shaker at home? Who is responsible for replenishing the dog's water bowl in your home? Likewise, Ms. Devereaux missed the opportunity to discuss the Word of the Week after the principal's announcements. She could have commented on the word and told students to try to catch her using it in the hours and days ahead.

## The Students

Students themselves are a source of language. When students listen to one another in the classroom, opportunities for language learning are increased—particularly when students have diverse backgrounds, experiences, and interests. A child whose family emigrated from Korea likely will offer more to his or her peers on topics related to Korean culture than a teacher who has limited knowledge of or few personal experiences with the culture. Likewise, the student who is an avid backpacker will enrich his or her peers' knowledge, and related language, of backpacking. We see this clearly in classrooms where students have time to contribute to the classroom dialog. For example, one of us was working with a group of fourth graders who were studying desert animals when a student spontaneously told his peers about a tortoise that he once owned. He enthusiastically described the reptile's habits, shared how he acquired the reptile, and talked about his feelings when the tortoise disappeared. He used words such as *enclosure, hibernate,* and *parasites.* His peers, genuinely interested in his experiences, asked questions that prompted extension and clarification.

A *sagacious* (wise) teacher ensures time for student discussion and capitalizes on students' expertise. He or she makes an effort to learn about students' experiences and interests and thoughtfully provides opportunities for them to share their knowledge with one another. Thus, students become sources of language input for each other.

The teacher who consciously supports vocabulary growth draws attention to students' sophisticated or specialized language use, as in these instances:

- Eleventh grader Melissa was conversing with her friends before class one morning when she commented that she was feeling querulous. Her teacher, who overheard the conversation, chuckled and replied, "What a great word, Melissa! *Querulous!* Wow! Why are you feeling irritable today? Didn't you get enough sleep?"

- Herman, a third grader, described a character in a novel as *impetuous*. "Great word choice, Herman," said his teacher. "Class, did you notice that word? *Impetuous*. Everyone say, 'Impetuous.' *Impetuous* means 'rash or impulsive.' Someone who is impetuous acts without thinking. Where do we see the character in this book behaving impetuously?"

- A sixth grader returned to school after summer break wearing braces … and using new terminology. She talked with others about her *malocclusion*, her *orthodontist*, and *fixed appliances*. Her teacher commented on the language that accompanied the student's experience. He wrote *orthodontist* on the board and told his students that *ortho* and *odons* come from Greek, meaning "straight" and "tooth," respectively. Thus, an *orthodontist* is someone who straightens teeth.

## The Text

A third very important model of language is written text. Because we discuss the powerful influence of the written word on language development in Chapter 3, we will only offer a brief preview here. In general, texts offer exposure to richer vocabulary than do oral language exchanges with adults. As conscious as we are of our word choices, speech is typically less sophisticated than the language of books. Thus, teachers must expose students to written materials and offer students ample time to read. In addition, teachers must read aloud to students regularly, taking time to discuss, among other things, some of the words in the text selection.

## The Curriculum

A fourth key source of language input is the curriculum. Learning specialized content vocabulary undergirds learning in every content area. How can students understand the Revolutionary War if they do not understand the terms *liberty*, *treason*, *taxation*, and *representation*? How can they understand fundamental life science concepts if they do not know *consumer*, *producer*, *decomposer*, *energy*, and *food chain*? How can they develop an aesthetic sense if they do not understand *texture*, *line*, *form*, *value*, and *space*? When teachers plan a content-area lesson, they should consider which specialized vocabulary words their students need to acquire as part of their learning. With new knowledge comes new language.

If the curriculum is shallow and offers no real learning opportunities, the vocabulary of the content becomes unnecessary; new words that might have become part of a student's linguistic repertoire do not. Think, for instance, about a primary-grade unit on pets. A superficial exploration of this topic may expose students to few, if any, new concepts or words. The students "learn" that many people own pets. Common pets include dogs, cats, hamsters, birds, and fish; some people have horses for pets. Students draw these animals and write simple sentences such as, "I wish I had a _____." or "My favorite pet is a _____. I like it because _____." This unit is hardly worthy of the instructional time.

On the other hand, imagine a primary-grade unit on organisms, specifically animals that have become domesticated and often are pets. Students learn that all organisms have basic needs, such as air, water, and food, and that they can only survive in a habitat where those needs are met. They learn about the characteristics of different animals that support their survival. For instance, they learn that mice have chisel-like teeth that allow them to eat seeds and nuts. They learn that horses have flat teeth that enable them to grind grass. They learn that dogs and cats have carnassials for killing and slicing. They learn terms like *herbivore*, *carnivore*, *omnivore*, and *specialized diet*. They hear the word *characteristics* multiple times over the course of the science unit, and they begin to use the word themselves. They examine photographs of familiar animals and look for specialized features. They use mirrors to look in their own mouths at the types of teeth they have. They use terms such as *canine teeth*, *incisors*, and *function*. They are exposed to the word *masticate*.

Unfortunately, even when the curriculum is rich, some teachers instill in their students the sense that the vocabulary is primarily to be learned (i.e., memorized) in order to pass a test rather than because it is central to the building of knowledge and to communicating that knowledge. In these classrooms, students may perform successfully at the moment—having temporarily memorized the terms—but they are not likely to own the words for long, if at all. Mrs. Jones, for example, treats social studies as a chore to be quickly accomplished. She points out the highlighted vocabulary in the text and asks students to read the chapter and answer the questions provided in the text. She quickly moves on to the next chapter. Her students see little value in the content and, although they may temporarily learn the related vocabulary in order to pass a test, they have little need to truly acquire and retain the new vocabulary. The words contributed little to their knowledge because their learning was superficial and temporary.

In other classrooms, words come to life as students question, investigate, and engage deeply with content. For instance, Mrs. Smith, who teaches next door to Mrs. Jones, breathes life into United States history with her passion for the subject matter, and her students eagerly respond to the topics under study. The content is explored in depth and connections are made among topics; repeated exposure to and meaningful use of content-specific vocabulary is the result. Students contribute to classroom discussions, share ideas and reactions, and ponder ideas. It is through meaningful experiences with the content that specialized vocabulary is developed and a deeper understanding of the content is achieved.

In sum, students must be exposed to rich vocabulary if their own vocabularies are to expand. They must be provided with an environment in which there is substantial linguistic input through the discourse of the teacher, peers, text, and the curriculum itself. However, input is only a part of the story. We turn now to the other part: language output.

# Language Output

Language output, or expressing oneself through language, is crucial for language development. Swain (1993) discussed this notion in relation to English language learners, but it is important for all children. Not only must students hear complex language and sophisticated vocabulary, they must also have opportunities to practice using it. As Blachowicz and Fisher (2005, 24) noted, "For students of all ages, … having lots of time for classroom talk is an essential aspect of encouraging informal word learning."

Think about your own experiences. You probably hear (and read) new words every day. Many of these words slip past you; that is, they do not become a part of your expressive vocabulary. However, when you have a need to use words—for example, as you summarize a news story for a friend or explain your son's foot injury to concerned colleagues—your awareness of word choices is heightened and you become more thoughtful about selecting words that convey precise meanings. You try out words you remember hearing and think about whether you are using them accurately. The same is true in the classroom. Students need opportunities to explain, discuss, and share—to communicate ideas that require the use of precise language.

Unfortunately, research shows that teachers do most of the talking in classrooms and that students' opportunities to talk are quite limited (National Center for Education Statistics 2003). When teachers do invite talk, they most typically engage in what has been identified as an I-R-E interchange. The teacher initiates (I) talk by asking a question, one student responds (R), and the teacher evaluates (E) the response (Cazden 1986). The I-R-E interchange is limited and limiting. In fact, notice that in this model, the teacher speaks two times for every one time a single student speaks. That particular student may not have the opportunity to speak again for some time. Thus, the teacher has far more opportunities to use language than any single student. Even worse, research suggests that as students move through the grade levels, their opportunities for talk decrease (Pinnell and Jaggar 2003).

Educators should provide many opportunities for students to engage in meaningful conversations with one another and with the teacher. Students who talk in pairs or small groups as they explore a topic in science, discuss their reactions to a shared educational experience, and converse to solve problems are exercising and developing their language. Teachers should ensure that students have opportunities to talk in a variety of settings and for a variety of purposes. Different settings and purposes elicit different language.

How can teachers encourage talk in the classroom? First, they must create a safe atmosphere for students to express themselves. Students must feel comfortable speaking with the teacher and with peers. They need to be confident that they will not be ridiculed if they misuse or mispronounce a word. The teacher has a responsibility to build a classroom community in which students respect and sincerely listen to one another. The relationships that the teacher forges with students and those established among the students will, in large measure, determine whether students are comfortable and willing to speak.

Second, teachers must create an environment that facilitates conversation. How you spatially arrange your classroom can facilitate or inhibit social interaction. Does the physical layout of the room allow for collaboration? For instance, are students' desks positioned in clusters or are they separated from one another? Do the desks face one another? Are there tables or other areas in the classroom where students can work together?

Third, teachers must give students time to talk. Is your day so jam-packed that there is no time for peer exploration and reflection on the content? Are you so busy filling the moments of students' school lives with listening to you and silently completing activity sheets that there are no opportunities for them to converse? Instead, students should be encouraged to work in table groups to solve problems and create projects and be prompted to turn to one another to review their learning. They should be invited to share reactions, questions, comments, and personal connections. As teachers prepare lessons, they should ensure that time for student talk is explicitly included in their plans and make sure that "student talk" doesn't mean that only the three or four most vocal students get to speak.

Fourth, teachers must provide students with reasons to talk. They must stimulate students' interest in the content, encourage students' questions, and provide them with experiences that are highly engaging and that arouse their curiosity. With genuine reasons to communicate, students will talk.

# Strategies for Encouraging Classroom Discourse

The remainder of this chapter is devoted to sharing strategies that engage students in talk; that is, they provide opportunities for language input and language output. Some of the strategies are easy "drop-ins" to any lesson you teach. They will work with any content area and at nearly any step in the instructional sequence. Others require more time and planning. What they all have in common is that they encourage high levels of student engagement with peers. In these strategies, most or all students will express their understandings of the content or their perspectives about an issue. Most or all students will share their experiences or ideas. Most or all will use the language of the subject matter. Sometimes students will share their thinking with one partner, sometimes with a small group, and sometimes with larger groups. We hope you will test these strategies in your own classroom and make thoughtful observations about the differences between the language experiences these strategies provide for students and the experiences provided by teachers who engage in the I-R-E classroom discussion pattern or who provide no opportunities for student talk at all.

## 1. Think-Pair-Share

Think-Pair-Share (Lyman 1981), a strategy that may be used in any content area, facilitates students' use of language as they first consider a question that the teacher has posed, briefly discuss their responses with partners, and then share their answers with the entire class. For example, when teaching about the Civil War, a teacher may stop and ask students to think of three important concepts from the lesson. Or the teacher may be more specific and ask students to state some of the causes of the war. After providing the students with a moment to think quietly, the teacher announces, "Pair," and students turn to their neighbors to talk about their responses. Finally, the teacher asks pairs to volunteer to share with the class some of the causes that they discussed. This strategy provides a break from teacher talk and allows students to articulate what they have learned. In their discussions, students use the language of the subject matter. In this example, words such as *abolition*, *confederacy*, and *secession*—ones they have heard from the teacher—begin to become part of their own repertoires because they have a chance to use them immediately. Note that this strategy contrasts with the I-R-E model in which the teacher initiates a response by posing a question, a single student responds, and the teacher evaluates or provides feedback. In Think-Pair-Share, all students talk.

In addition to providing a structure for students to respond to questions as a review of content, Think-Pair-Share may be used to facilitate students' thinking about connections between the content and students' lives or other content. For instance, if a teacher is about to begin a lesson or unit of study on animals' defenses, he or she may ask students to think about any self-protective behavior they have witnessed in their pets or in wild animals. Then students talk in pairs about their observations, and finally, they share with the class.

## 2. 10:2 Lecture

A strategy similar to Think-Pair-Share is the 10:2 Lecture. This strategy is described by Brechtel (2001) as a means for providing English language learners with an opportunity to practice language, but we believe it is useful for all learners. The idea is that after approximately every 10 minutes of instruction, students should be provided with two minutes of oral processing time. In other words, students should turn to a partner and discuss what they have learned. This paired response time provides a risk-free environment for testing understanding of new ideas and information and prompts the students to use oral language to express and clarify their understandings. The 10:2 Lecture does not include the think time that is a step in Think-Pair-Share, but it can easily be modified to include think time prior to paired discussion. One advantage of this strategy is that it requires frequent pauses in instruction for student talk, and the name itself—10:2 Lecture—is a good reminder of the importance of providing students with frequent opportunities to talk about what they are learning.

## 3. Numbered Heads Together

Numbered Heads Together is a cooperative learning strategy that increases students' opportunities to talk. In this strategy, described by Kagan (1994), the teacher asks questions about the content and, rather than call on individuals to respond, he or she has the students meet in small groups of four to discuss the answer. Students are numbered off so there is a one, two, three, and four in each group. After allowing the students time to discuss the answer to the question, the teacher randomly selects a number from one to four (perhaps using an overhead spinner) and asks all the students with that number to raise their hands. Then she calls on one of the students whose hand is raised.

This strategy promotes high levels of engagement because

the students work together to generate a response to the question, and their task is to ensure that everyone in their group knows the answer. All students realize they may be selected to articulate the answer for their group and therefore are motivated to participate. Kagan contrasted Numbered Heads Together with the more typical classroom exchanges we described earlier and noted that the traditional approach can promote negative interdependence as students compete against one another for the opportunity to answer the question. Numbered Heads Together instead promotes positive interdependence while also promoting individual accountability. Furthermore, because students work in small groups to craft a response, we believe the strategy offers students who otherwise might not have volunteered to respond the opportunity to share their thoughts and practice using academic language.

Teacher questions may range from those that require a single brief response (e.g., "What is the capital of Wyoming?") to those that require an explanation (e.g., "Explain how to convert improper fractions to mixed numbers.") and those that invite diverse responses (e.g., "Give three examples of energy you saw on the way to school today."). Of course, the more open-ended the question, the more talk that will occur in the group.

As we noted before, providing students with brief think time before talking with peers allows them to gather their thoughts and thus increases the likelihood that they will have something to contribute to the conversation. Even if some students have less to say in their groups, the odds are one in four that their numbers will be selected and so they generally listen actively and rehearse the response so they can successfully represent their group if called upon.

4. **Learning Circles**

Based on the literature circles described by Daniels (1994), learning circles may be established to provide a vehicle for discussion of content. Learning circles are formed by small groups of students who meet periodically to share ideas about the content they have been studying. Each student has a different role in the circle, and so all students have something unique to contribute to the group conversation. Roles vary widely and may be determined by students or the teacher. For instance, one student may be a summarizer, reviewing for the group what has been taught. Another student may be a word catcher, reminding the group of the specialized vocabulary that has been introduced. He or she may share a dictionary definition of each word and the contexts in which the teacher (or other source) used the words. A third student may be a questioner, bringing to the group several questions for discussion. A fourth member of the group may serve as an illustrator, drawing in response to the content and then sharing with group members the illustration and eliciting their reactions. Roles may also include a connector who thinks about and makes connections between the content and the students' lives, a text, or the world. Learning circles provide an authentic reason for students to use language in order to share with one another what they have learned and to further explore subject matter.

5. **Powerful Passages and Significant Sentences**

In *Literature-Based Reading Activities* (H. K. Yopp and Yopp 2006), we described a strategy that encourages talk after students have read a selection from a work of literature or a content-area textbook. The teacher prompts the students to identify a powerful passage (or, if the teacher prefers, a significant sentence) they wish to share with their peers. Students read their passages aloud to several partners, one at a time, and explain why they chose the passages. In other words, they share their passages with several peers in succession and provide the rationale for their selections. When we have used this strategy with students ranging from the elementary to university level, we have noticed that students at all levels become more fluent in their reading of the passage and more articulate and detailed in their explanations with each sharing.

This simple strategy may be used with groups as they read the same text (e.g., after reading a section in their social studies text) or as they read different texts (e.g., after a silent reading period during which they read self-selected books). When all students have read the same text, they are interested in comparing their passage selections with one another. Because there is no "correct" selection, students engage in authentic conversations about their choices; they demonstrate interest in the variety of passages and their understanding of the text deepens as they discuss their choices. When students have read different texts, they provide their partners with contextual information about the passages, perhaps summarizing the events in the story to this point or describing a character's personality prior to sharing their passages. Thus, the talk that surrounds the sharing of the passages is plentiful.

6. **Inquiry Lessons**

   Inquiry lessons engage students in investigations to satisfy their own curiosities and answer their own questions. The lessons prompt exploration and discovery. Students have their hands on objects, materials, or resources; they seek information; and they generate and test hypotheses as they look for explanations and solutions. Because vocabulary acquisition occurs most easily in context when students care about the topics, inquiry lessons are ideal for promoting students' purposeful use of language and developing students' language.

   Many teachers are skilled at designing lessons that spark students' active search for knowledge. In science, for example, they demonstrate startling events, such as a peeled hard-boiled egg being sucked into a small-mouthed bottle.

Students are surprised by the demonstration, ask questions of the teacher and each other, offer tentative explanations, request replications of the event, and look to expert sources to seek explanations for their observations—all the while engaged in purposeful discussion about the unexpected event. Other teachers supply a variety of materials related to the curriculum, such as seeds or magnets, and allow students to explore them with peers. In social studies, teachers invite students to view a range of print and nonprint resources, such as texts, images, and other artifacts related to their study of hunter-gatherer societies. As students interact with the resources, they generate questions and the teacher supports them in refining those questions and conducting investigations related to them.

Students often have strong affective responses when they observe discrepant events, handle materials, and view interesting images. These responses are usually accompanied by language, as students spontaneously express their thoughts and feelings or share their knowledge and personal experiences. Teachers can capitalize on student interest and further students' language development by creating environments that support inquiry and encouraging students to work together to pursue the answers to their questions.

### 7. Wordless Picture Books

You read about Chad's positive experience with a wordless picture book in our "Introduction: First Words" section. Wordless picture books are rich in images but contain very little or no text. They are typically narratives; that is, the illustrations convey a story. One of our favorite wordless picture books is Tomie dePaola's (1978) humorous *Pancakes for Breakfast*. This book tells the story of a woman who awakens early one morning craving pancakes. As viewers turn the pages, they see her futile efforts to obtain the necessary ingredients. The illustrations in wordless picture books such as *Pancakes for Breakfast* provide rich detail that supports comprehension, and they beg for students to use oral language to share what they see.

Wordless picture books may be used with any age group. With young children, teachers might begin by talking about the illustrations in detail and using precise and complex language to share the story the pictures tell (e.g., "On this page, we see the sun is rising. It casts a warm, red glow across the hills and through the woman's curtainless window. It looks like early morning in the countryside."). Then teachers invite the children to tell what they see as they work their way through the pages together (e.g., "Ah! What is happening on this page?"). If multiple copies of the book are available, they may be distributed to the students, who then revisit the book and tell the story to one another, changing it as they wish to reflect their views of the story.

Older students may be encouraged to work with partners to create a story based on the illustrations. All students should be prompted to provide details to foster oral language: What is the setting? What words might be used to describe the hills? What can we tell about the character by the expression on his or her face? What is he or she thinking and doing? Why is the character doing what he or she is doing?

A meaningful extension of sharing wordless picture books is to have students create original works and share them with one another.

Teachers can alter books with text to make wordless picture books. The books must have illustrations that convey the story sufficiently so that the words are not necessary. The teacher covers the text using strips of paper or sticky notes and shares the book as he or she would a wordless picture book.

Some of our favorite wordless picture books include the following:

- Aliki. *Tabby*. New York: HarperCollins, 1995.

- Baker, Jeannie. *Home*. New York: Greenwillow, 2004.

- Bang, Molly. *The Grey Lady and the Strawberry Snatcher*. New York: Four Winds Press, 1980.

- Carle, Eric. *Do You Want to Be My Friend*? New York: Philomel Books, 1988.

- Crews, Donald. *Freight Train*. New York: Greenwill Books, 1978.

- Day, Alexandra. *Good Dog, Carl*. New York: Simon & Schuster, 1986.

- Hutchins, Pat. *Rosie's Walk*. New York: Aladdin Paperbacks, 2005.

- Jenkins, Steve. *Looking Down*. Boston: Houghton Mifflin, 1997.

- Keats, Ezra Jack. *Clementina's Cactus*. New York: Viking, 1999.

- Lui, Jae-Soo. *Yellow Umbrella*. La Jolla, CA: Kane/Miller Book Publishers, 2002.

- Mayer, Mercer, and Marianna Mayer. *A Boy, a Dog, a Frog, and a Friend*. New York: Dial Press, 1971.

- Rothman, Eric. *Time Flies*. New York: Dell Dragonfly, 2003.

- Spier, Peter. *Peter Spier's Rain*. Garden City, NY: Doubleday, 1982.

- Van Allsburg, Chris. *Mysteries of Harris Burdick*. Boston: Houghton Mifflin, 1984.

- Wiesner, David. *Tuesday*. New York: Clarion, 1991.

8. **Photo Review**

   Photographs of students engaging in learning activities may also be used as prompts for oral language. The teacher takes photos of students during a lesson or unit of study and later distributes copies of the photos to the class. Students are then asked to closely examine the photos and talk with one another about what they see and remember about the lesson. The teacher encourages the students to be specific and use words that are important to the content. He or she may even identify particular words, writing them on the board or distributing word cards, that he or she hopes to hear the students use. In this way, the teacher promotes the students' use of academic vocabulary.

   For instance, as part of a mathematics unit on graphing, a fifth-grade teacher might have students work in small groups to gather data on how high a ball bounces when dropped from four feet. Students measure the height of the first bounce and the subsequent bounces and observe that the height of the bounce changes over time, decreasing with each bounce. Students record the data and then work in teams to display the data on graphs. The graphs are posted in the classroom. The teacher takes digital photos throughout the investigation and again as students record and post their data. The teacher selects representative photos and prints four of them on a single page, makes a copy for each group, and the next day, asks students to meet in their same groups. The teacher distributes the photo pages and gives each group a set of word cards. On each card is written one of the following words: *investigation, line graph, x-axis, y-axis,* and *scale.* The teacher tells the students that he or she will be listening for them to use these words as they discuss the data with one another. The photos and word cards serve to spark the students' memories and promote a high level of engagement because the students are likely to be eager to talk about what they see themselves and their classmates doing in the photos.

A primary-grade teacher might take photos of his or her students engaged in a music lesson in which they explore different types of instruments and learn a system for classification. Photos include students beating on drums and tambourines, examining a guitar, and experimenting with recorders. The teacher hands one of the students the camera and asks the student to take a photo of him or her playing the trumpet. After photos are printed and distributed, students talk with one another about what they learned. The teacher writes the terms *classification, string, wind, brass,* and *percussion* on the board and asks students to use them in their discussions. After a few moments of student talk, the teacher asks for volunteers to share with the entire class. The teacher applauds their use of the terminology.

A junior high school science teacher might share photos of equipment in his or her lab as a review at the end of the first month of school. The teacher provides sets of the photos to small groups of students and asks them to talk with one another about the names, purposes, and any experiences (including in-class activities) they had with each piece of equipment. The photos are then projected on a large screen and a brief whole-class discussion is held.

9. **Sketch to Stretch**

Adapted from Harste, Short, and Burke (1988), Sketch to Stretch is intended to stretch students' thinking and promote discussion as students sketch their understanding of the content after reading a text selection, hearing a lecture, or participating in a learning experience. Sketches, quickly rendered, may be literal or symbolic, narrowly or broadly focused, and elaborate or simple. After allowing a few minutes for sketching, the teacher prompts students to meet in small groups to share their work. Students talk about what they see in one another's sketches before they offer detailed explanations of their own drawings. The teacher may circulate throughout the room and record key words he or she hears in students' discussions, later commenting on their usage of important vocabulary.

Although Sketch to Stretch is typically used after students have engaged with content, it may be used before students engage with content as a means of activating their background knowledge on a topic. For instance, just prior to studying the topic, a teacher might ask his or her students to sketch images that come to mind when they hear the word *erosion*. Thus, students' background knowledge (including relevant vocabulary) is activated. Again, the teacher may wish to comment on students' vocabularies or use their discussions as a springboard for introducing key vocabulary.

## 10. Capture the Content

The teachers in the science department at the high school that two of our children attend ask the students each week to tell a parent or other adult three concepts they learned during the week. The teachers provide a standard form on which the parent records what the student says, and then the parent signs the form. The student submits a form each Friday. We were pleased with the important attempt to facilitate school-home connections, and we have been struck by the amount of conversation that occurs as our children work to articulate their learning. We notice that they sometimes grope for the appropriate terminology, and they occasionally search for the right word in their notes or textbooks. We often request clarification and explanation so that we can put into writing what our children are communicating. Through this exercise, our children have to think about the content, consider the important concepts, and use language to express their learning.

Here is an example of a conversation Peter and his mother had about a concept from his ninth-grade biology class. Notice that his mother requested clarification and assistance from her son so she could clearly articulate a concept on the form.

Mom: Okay Peter, I'm ready. What's one of the concepts you discussed in class this week?

Peter: Fungi are cleaners of the planet.

Mom: I'm not sure what you mean.

Peter: Well, fungi break down dead animals, for one thing.

Mom: Oh, I get it. Interesting. How shall I write that?

Peter: Something like fungi are decomposers, that they break down dead organisms, that if they didn't, all the dead plants and animals would take up a lot of space on the earth.

Mom: Fascinating. Sounds like they serve a very useful purpose. Help me put all that you said in a sentence. You said a few things. "Fungi are decomposers ..."

Peter: Okay, you can write: "As decomposers, fungi clean the environment of dead organisms, breaking them down into useable nutrients for other life."

Mom: That's great. You even added a little more information!

Peter: Mom, can you imagine what would happen if there were no fungi? Think about all the dead leaves, animals, and other waste that would pile up on the planet.

Note how the science teachers' simple request that students talk to their family members about three concepts learned during the week sparked a great deal of language from the student. Peter thought about the concepts he had learned, used language to verbalize the concepts, and revised his language to help his mother understand and record his thoughts. This strategy can be implemented at any grade level and is a wonderful way to get students talking at home about what they are learning at school.

## 11. Mystery Bags

Mystery Bags can be used to spark conversations about a topic. The teacher prepares a bag by inserting objects that are related to the content of an upcoming lesson or unit. For instance, if kindergarteners are going to explore tools for measuring time, the teacher might include a stopwatch, wrist watch, alarm clock, calendar, metronome, pocket watch, hourglass, and small sundial. If third graders are going to explore principles of light, the teacher might place a flashlight, mirror, container of water, and glasses in the bag. If eighth graders are beginning a unit on work (i.e., the scientific meaning of this word), the teacher might place a nutcracker, wheel, screw, and scissors in the bag. Small groups of students are each given a bag (which may or may not contain identical items) and either at the teacher's signal or on their own, students remove one object at a time from the bag. As each object is removed, the students' task is to identify and talk about the object. They are encouraged to draw on their experiences with or knowledge about the object. If a wheel is pulled from the bag, for instance, students share what they know about its use. Then another item is taken from the bag. Students again identify it and discuss it. They also talk about how it might be related to the first item. Why would both items be in the same bag? The mystery surrounding the bag, the opportunity to handle objects, and the time to talk informally generally facilitates interest and conversation.

## 12. Response Cards

This strategy engages students in talking about content from a variety of perspectives. The teacher prepares for the activity by gathering colored index cards, making decisions about the tasks he or she wants the students to perform, and recording those tasks on the cards. For example, the teacher might write "Question" on all of the yellow cards, "Connect" on all of the blue cards, and "Summarize" on all of the green cards. Then he or she randomly distributes the cards to the students, one card per student.

As the teacher reads, lectures, shows a video, or provides some other instructional input, he or she invites the students to think about the content from the perspective of a questioner, connector, or summarizer, depending on the card they received. Those with yellow cards think about questions they have about the content, those with blue cards think about connections they can make between the content and their lives or other material they have learned, and those with green cards think about how they would summarize the information being presented.

The teacher pauses in his or her instruction after several minutes and asks the students with the yellow cards to meet with one or two other students with a yellow card and, as a team, generate questions. Likewise, he or she asks the students with the blue cards to gather in small groups and those with green cards to meet with one or two others. After giving students a few minutes of talk time, the teacher asks the students to share their questions, connections, and summaries with the whole group. Then the teacher continues with his or her instruction and, at an appropriate point, stops and again asks the students to meet with partners and engage in their assigned tasks.

After several opportunities to question, connect, or summarize, the teacher tells the students to trade their cards for one of a different color. The students engage in the new tasks and meet with different classmates as they talk about the content of the lesson.

The response cards strategy is generally a highly motivating experience that stimulates considerable discussion about the topic and provides students with an opportunity to think—and talk—about the content from more than one perspective.

13. **Jigsaw**

The Jigsaw strategy has a long history and numerous variations (Kagan 1994). It is an approach to instruction that involves the students becoming experts in some portion of the learning material. Students form groups and each member is assigned or selects one section of the material to be learned. The students gather information about their portions of the material, often using text resources, and then teach the information to their groupmates. Jigsaw provides an outstanding opportunity for students to deeply process content and use specialized content vocabulary to teach their peers.

14. **Four Corners**

Four Corners gets students out of their seats and talking with classmates about important content or ideas. The teacher asks a question or makes a statement and then sends the students to the four corners of the classroom to respond to the prompt. For example, the teacher might ask students to think about whether they agree with the following statement after reading *A Single Shard* by Linda Sue Park (2001): "Tree-ear was foolish to carry the potter's vases to the royal court." After giving the students a few moments to think about this statement, the teacher asks them to go to the corner of the room that reflects their reaction to the statement. The corners are designated *Strongly Agree*, *Agree*, *Disagree*, and *Strongly Disagree*. In their corners, the students discuss their ideas about the statement. Then the teacher invites students in each corner to share the group's thinking about the statement. Sometimes teachers prepare and ask for responses to several statements before students begin moving to corners so that after discussing the first statement, students can travel to the next corner—at a signal—to discuss their responses to the next statement.

A variation of this strategy is to assign the students to corners. After the students have learned about changes to the earth's surface, for example, the teacher might randomly assign students to corners labeled *Earthquake*, *Erosion and Weathering*, *Landslides*, and *Volcanic Eruptions*. Students talk about what they know about each of these change processes and then summarize the group's discussion for the class.

# Conclusion

Language learning cannot occur without exposure to language, and it is enhanced by opportunities to use language. In this chapter, we discussed the importance of providing students with plentiful opportunities for both language input and language output. Students need to be exposed to language through rich and meaningful interactions with their teacher, peers, text, and the curriculum. Teachers need to be intentional and deliberate about providing these sources of input. Similarly, teachers must carefully plan for many daily opportunities for students to engage in discussion with others in order to give them experiences with the words they are learning as well as reasons to learn new words.

We opened this chapter with a strategy that we describe in Chapter 5. This strategy, called Possible Sentences, asked you to think about what you already know about several terms and the relationships among them and to take an educated guess at how the terms might be used in a sentence. We hope the strategy stretched your thinking and also sparked your curiosity about the words. We encourage you to revisit the sentences you generated and think about how you would revise them now that you have read the chapter. You might also locate them in this chapter and see how we used them.

# Think About It!

1. Think about the vocabulary that your students encounter in your classroom. Audiotape yourself for 10 minutes one day. Listen to the recording and jot down the sophisticated or specialized terminology you used. Later, record yourself again with the goal of using even more of these words. Listen to the recording, jot down the rich words, and compare the number with your first recording.

2. List each of the ways you ensure that students have time to talk. Share the most successful way with a colleague.

3. As noted in this chapter, students need a safe atmosphere in which to express themselves. How do you establish a safe atmosphere for your English language learners?

# Chapter 3

# Promoting Wide Reading

## Reading Questionnaire

Answer the following questions about your reading practices.

1. What is the name of a book you are currently reading or recently read for pleasure?

   _____

   _____

2. How did you select this book? (Check all that apply.)

   _____ A friend told me about it.

   _____ I have read other works by the author.

   _____ The book cover was appealing and the description on the jacket was interesting.

   _____ I like this genre.

   _____ It won a book club award, and I often enjoy books recommended by this club.

   _____ It was a gift.

   _____ Other: _____

3. What is the name of the last book you read aloud to your students?

   _____

4. How would you describe your typical read-aloud session? (Check all that apply.)

_____ I introduce the book and read it from cover to cover with no discussion.

_____ I ask comprehension questions after I finish reading the book aloud.

_____ I show the pictures before or as I read each page of the book.

_____ I interject comments and questions during my reading.

_____ I allow students to comment before, during, and after I read.

_____ I make the book available to students after I read it to them.

5. List three ways you try to promote independent reading in your classroom.

_____

_____

_____

_____

*"One must be drenched in words, literally soaked in them, to have the right ones form themselves into the proper pattern at the right moment."*

—Hart Crane

There is general agreement that, on average, students add approximately 3,000 words a year to their reading vocabularies between the third and twelfth grades. Direct instruction accounts for only about a few hundred new words each year (Cunningham 2005). How do students gain the additional words? We answered this question in Chapter 1 when we stated that students learn huge numbers of words incidentally—that is, through everyday experiences with language. In Chapter 2, we discussed the incidental learning that occurs through rich oral language experiences. In this chapter, we turn to what Stahl and Nagy (2006) stated is the single most powerful factor in vocabulary growth and what Cunningham and Stanovich (2003) argue is the prime contributor to individual differences in children's vocabularies: wide reading.

In order to understand why reading is a powerful means of learning new words, let us examine the difference between oral and written language. Perhaps the most frequently cited research in this area is the work of Hayes and Ahrens (1988). These researchers analyzed words that appeared in a variety of contexts: written texts ranging from preschool materials to scientific abstracts, adult speech in various settings, and television, including children's programs and prime-time adult programs. Based on a frequency ranking developed by Carroll, Davies, and Richman (1971), words from these sources were analyzed in terms of their rarity. That is, the words were ranked according to how frequently they occur in the English language. As you might expect, text materials varied in their use of rare words. Scientific abstracts contained the greatest number of rare words per thousand, followed in order by newspapers, popular magazines, adult books, comic books, children's books, and preschool books. In other words, the researchers found that the language of scientific abstracts is more sophisticated and includes more low-frequency, or rare, words than the other printed materials, which include proportionately more common words. Does this finding surprise you? Probably not. What might surprise you, however, is the finding that all types of written materials except preschool books contained proportionately more rare words than all types of television programs and all adult speech situations studied. Even children's books contained more rare words than any of the oral language situations.

Why might this be so? One reason is that in oral settings, such as the adult speech situations, speakers must quickly access words in order to hold the floor or keep the conversation moving. Common words are more quickly accessed in the brain than rare words (Marshalek, Lohman, and Snow in Cunningham 2005) and therefore are used in greater proportions. Unlike speakers, writers have time to search their vocabularies—as well as a variety of resources—and thus can be more selective in their word choices.

A second explanation for the greater use of rare words in written language is that oral language situations are highly contextualized. Because writers do not have the benefit of face-to-face communication with their readers that allows for gestures, facial expressions, intonation, and feedback, they must carefully select words that accurately convey their messages. Written texts by necessity contain more specific and precise language than oral language exchanges.

This greater use of rare words makes written materials an excellent source of new words. Students are more likely to come across words that are not part of their current vocabularies when they read (or are read to) than when they engage in or listen to conversations. A wise teacher ensures that his or her students have extensive experiences with written language, both through reading and being read to, so they have many opportunities to learn new words.

Although research demonstrates that students of all ages and abilities learn words through reading, Cunningham (2005) identified several factors that influence the process. These include the following:

- **The difficulty of the text and the student's level of comprehension:** The text should be matched to the student's level of comprehension. Students are less likely to learn new words from materials that they find too difficult or too easy.

- **The word's conceptual difficulty:** The more difficult the word (e.g., *democracy*), the less likely a student will learn it from context. Less conceptually difficult words (e.g., *president*) are easier to learn.

- **How vital the word is to understanding:** The more important the word is to the ideas in the text, the more likely the student will learn it.

- **The informativeness of the context:** The more information provided by the surrounding text, the more likely the student will learn the word.

- **The number of times the word is encountered:** Repeated encounters with the word increase the likelihood that the student will learn it.

These factors are important to remember as you plan reading experiences for your students. And planning for wide-reading experiences is vital. As Kamil and Hiebert (2005) noted, the powerful vocabulary development that arises from reading may be incidental, but the reading experiences offered in classrooms reflect intentions on the part of teachers. Teachers must be thoughtful and deliberate about providing their students with opportunities to engage with written language. They must plan many and varied opportunities for students to read—accompanied by important reasons to read—and they must share books by reading them aloud.

The notion of wide reading is important. If students only read one genre or one topic, their exposure will be limited to the language of that genre and topic. Although extensive reading on a single topic is valuable and offers depth, breadth is also crucial for expanding vocabulary.

In the remainder of this chapter, we discuss independent reading by students and reading aloud on the part of teachers as two important vehicles for vocabulary growth. We also provide a number of strategies for promoting and engaging students in powerful reading experiences.

# Independent Reading

Independent reading refers to the reading that students do by themselves without support from the teacher. Several studies provide evidence that independent reading is related to vocabulary growth. We briefly describe two here.

Nagy and Herman (1987), in an expansion of an earlier study, examined how students in grades three, five, and seven were able to use context to learn difficult words while reading expository and narrative material. They found growth in vocabulary at all grade and ability levels. Based on this and earlier research, they stated that regular and wide reading must be seen as the major avenue of large-scale, long-term vocabulary growth.

In another carefully controlled study, this time of fourth-, fifth-, and sixth-grade students, Cunningham and Stanovich (1991) found that the amount of reading students do is likely a significant contributor to increased vocabulary development. Of special importance is the fact that the study took careful steps to control the effect of age, intelligence, and decoding ability.

Not surprisingly, there is also research that reveals that there is great variation in the amount of reading students actually do. Anderson, Wilson, and Fielding (1988), for example, asked fifth graders to report on their out-of-school activities and then determined the number of minutes they spent reading each day. Averages ranged from zero minutes to 65 minutes per day. Although some students read quite a bit, far too many students did not. In fact, there was a dramatic drop in average reading time from students at the 99th percentile, who read 65 minutes per day, to those at the 90th percentile, who read 21 minutes per day, and frighteningly, those at the 50th percentile, who read a mere 4.6 minutes per day. If students read at an average rate, the researchers calculated that students who read 65 minutes per day encountered 4,358,000 words in a year and those who read 4.6 minutes per day encountered 432,000 words per year, or approximately 10 percent of what their enthusiastic peers read. Students below the 50th percentile, of course, read far less and were exposed to far fewer words. Students at the 10th percentile, for instance, encountered the same number of words over the course of a year that students in the 90th percentile encountered in two days! The cumulative differences in exposure to words are staggering.

We view this and similar research as a call to action. Extensive reading is known to support literacy development, and—of particular interest to us in this context—it is recognized to promote vocabulary growth. Indeed, vocabulary knowledge is said to be a direct result of how much a student reads (Shaywitz 2003). All teachers must commit themselves to providing opportunities, resources, and reasons for their students to engage in wide reading.

## Strategies for Promoting Independent Reading

If students are to read widely, they must be guided to see the personal value of reading. Pressley and Hilden (2002) asserted that while there are far too many factors beyond a teacher's control, motivating students to read is not one of them. Just about everyone has a "Zone of Curiosity" (Day 1982). When in this zone, individuals have personally valuable questions and search for information and answers related to these questions. Guthrie and Wiggins (2000) discussed "engaged reading," defining it as the merger of motivation and thoughtfulness. They indicated that engaged readers are intrinsically motivated and that teachers can enhance the engagement process by developing classroom environments that promote powerful, relevant literature. The following are strategies that guide students to see the value of reading in their lives and enhance their desire to read.

### 1. Model Enjoyment of Reading

An important yet simple strategy for promoting wide reading is for teachers to be readers themselves. Teachers who read for pleasure, who talk to students about books, and who share interesting or funny passages from books they are reading convey an enthusiasm that can influence students' reading attitudes and behaviors. Teachers are important role models for students and must communicate through their actions that reading is a meaningful and enjoyable experience (Gambrell 1996, 2007).

Sadly, not all teachers are enthusiastic readers, and a recent study found that approximately half of the prospective teachers surveyed associated no or very little enjoyment with reading and did little leisure reading (Applegate and Applegate 2004). Arguing that to create students who are highly-engaged readers, we need teachers who are highly-engaged readers, Dreher (2003) proposed that teachers participate in book talks at faculty meetings or establish after-school teacher book clubs. The eagerness to read generated by interacting with colleagues about books will transfer to the classroom, where students will see how important reading is to the teacher. If teachers want students to read widely, they must be active readers themselves.

## 2. Introduce Popular Authors

One of the authors of this book survived the first year of teaching by reading aloud E. B. White's *Charlotte's Web* (2001). Each day, before a chapter was read, students were guided to ask questions and make predictions about what they thought was going to happen. Some days, questions and predictions took longer than the actual reading. There was little doubt that the students were well within their zones of curiosity. At the end of the day, students wrote what they suspected would happen to Wilbur the next day. They went home excited and came to school excited. As the class moved through the book, students were thrilled to discover that White had also written *Stuart Little* (1974), a book about a mouse born into a human family. When *Stuart Little* was put on display in the classroom, students' movement toward the book best resembled a stampede. In addition, children wanted to learn more about spiders, the webs they spin, their sizes, and, of course, pigs, rats, and other farm animals. Rich reading naturally followed. Through Charlotte, Stuart, and their teacher, students quickly discovered that books provide answers to important questions. Wide reading was a very natural result. Of course, White is not the only author who has helped teachers motivate students to read. The authors listed below have written one or more popular series of books. As with *Charlotte's Web* and *Stuart Little*, after one book has been enjoyed, it is the rare child who does not want to read other books by the author. The motivation to read every book in a series is significant. The *Harry Potter* books are impressive examples. The following is certainly not an exhaustive list, but it does represent a rich sample of popular authors whose works are available to teachers looking to motivate students to read extensively.

## Early Elementary

- Arnold Lobel—*Frog and Toad* books
- Peggy Parish—*Amelia Bedelia* books
- H. A. Rey—*Curious George* books
- Ludwig Bemelmans—*Madeline* books
- Jan and Stan Berenstain—*Berenstain Bears* books
- Norman Bridwell—*Clifford, the Big Red Dog* books
- Laura Numeroff—*If You Give a . . .* books
- Doreen Cronin—*Click, Clack, Moo: Cows that Type* and other animal books
- Marc Brown—*Arthur* books
- Kay Thompson—*Eloise* books
- Kevin Henkes—*Lilly* books

## Middle and Upper Elementary

- James Howe—*Bunnicula* books
- Beverly Cleary—*Henry and Beezus* and *Ramona* books
- Jon Sciezka—*Fairytale* books
- Lynne Reid Banks—*Indian in the Cupboard* books
- Donald J. Sobol—*Encyclopedia Brown* books
- Judy Blume—*Fudge* books
- William Steig—His original *Shrek!* book inspired the Shrek books and movies
- Paula Danzinger—*Amber Brown* books
- J. K. Rowling—*Harry Potter* books
- Lemony Snicket—*Unfortunate Events* books
- Lloyd Alexander—*Chronicles of Prydain* books
- Brian Jacques—*Redwall* books

## Middle and High School

- Christopher Paul Curtis—*The Watsons Go to Birmingham—1963, Bud Not Buddy, Elijah of Buxton*

- Linda Sue Park—*When My Name was Keoko, A Single Shard, Seesaw Girl* and other stories set in Korea

- Walter Dean Myers—*Monster, Somewhere in the Darkness, Scorpions* and other books depicting African American experiences

- Will Hobbs—*Far North, Bearstone, Ghost Canoe* and other outdoor adventure stories

- Nancy Farmer—*The Ear, the Eye, and the Arm: A Novel; A Girl Named Disaster; The House of the Scorpion* and other largely futuristic and science fiction works

- Avi—*Crispin: The Cross of Lead, Nothing But the Truth, The True Confessions of Charlotte Doyle* and the *I Witness* series

- Jerry Spinelli—*Stargirl, Wringer, Maniac McGee, Milkweed* and others

- Stephen King—*The Shining, The Dead Zone* and other works of horror and science fiction

- James Patterson—the *Maximum Ride* books

3. **Share Books Related to Important Events and Life Experiences**

Significant news events, field trips, birthdays, holidays, the changing of the seasons, hot days, rainy days, guest speakers, and other experiences that students view as special occur throughout the school year. All are authentic reasons to read widely—not just fiction and informational books, but poetry as well. A trip to a community arboretum can inspire students to read about plants. A presentation by a geologist can motivate students to learn more about rocks. A hurricane in another region of the world can prompt questions that are answered in books. Conversely, books can prompt, inspire, or generate reasons for classroom experiences. Teachers who read McGovern's *Stone Soup* (1986), for example, can have students make a version of the "stone" soup in the book. This activity can be followed by the sharing of food poems such as "Peanut-Butter Sandwich" and "Recipe for a Hippopotamus Sandwich" from *Where the Sidewalk Ends* (Silverstein 2004). When teachers link books to the world that the students are experiencing, students will come to see that books have direct connections to their lives.

*Bibliotherapy* is the use of books to help students cope with the complexities of life. If students feel they are too tall, short, wide, or thin, there are books that can help them better understand issues and solutions and, most importantly, come to understand that they are not alone in their feelings and concerns. At any age, but especially for the very young, the beginning of the school year and the search for friends can be a stressful time, particularly for those new to the school. Reading and discussing Hallinan's *That's What a Friend Is* (1977) is a powerful way to guide young children to gain new friends and help them see books as relevant and valuable. When students see that books can provide them with solutions to problems that are significant in their lives, they will come to appreciate the personal value of literature. This can lead to wide reading.

4. **Use Text Sets**

Text sets, a collection of books related to a common topic or theme, can provide students with repeated exposure to powerful and important vocabulary. Creating a learning unit where students read and write extensively about an area of interest helps students internalize key vocabulary. For example, initiated by the first rainy day of the school year, the teacher can read to students Wood's *The Napping House* (2004). This is a wonderfully illustrated, warm, and gentle book dealing with a lazy, rainy day. If you would like to make a rainy day a little more exciting, read Barrett's *Cloudy with a Chance of Meatballs* (1982). With teacher guidance, students will want to learn more about rain. Make available and encourage students to independently read *It's Raining Cats and Dogs: All Kinds of Weather and Why We Have It* (Branley 1987), *Flash, Crash, Rumble, and Roll* (Branley 1999), and *The Cloud Book* (dePaola 1984). In each of these books, students repeatedly encounter such words as *precipitation, drizzle*, and *droplets*. In addition, encourage students to read weather-related poems such as "Rain" and "Lazy Jane" from Silverstein's *Where the Sidewalk Ends* (2004). An excellent source of additional weather-related poems is *The Random House Book of Poetry for Children* (Prelutsky 1983).

The possibilities with text sets are almost endless. Text sets can center on any content area, time period, historical event, individual, or theme. Nonfiction, historical fiction, picture books, audiotapes or files, brochures and maps, websites, pictures, charts, visits by authorities, field trips, interviews, newspapers, and magazines are all appropriate sources of information. When possible, text selections should include material of varying reading levels and material that provides different political, gender, and cultural perspectives of the same event. This provides students with a richer view of the topic and helps them come to understand the role of vocabulary in clearly communicating important concepts.

Text sets are a particularly effective way to expose students to new words for at least two reasons. First, as we noted above, they provide repeated exposure to important words, increasing the likelihood that students will learn them. Second, they provide rich and diverse contexts for the words, supporting increasingly complex understandings of the words.

## 5. Provide Opportunities and Encouragement

Students will not engage in wide reading if they are not provided with time to read. It is therefore essential that teachers plan regular opportunities for students to read at school and encourage them to read at home. One popular practice is to schedule a sustained silent reading time during the school day. Known as SSR (sustained silent reading), DEAR (drop everything and read), or by a variety of other acronyms, this practice involves providing time each day, perhaps 20 minutes, for students to read books of their own choosing. Students must read but are not required to complete book reports or other formal responses. The purpose of silent reading time is to engage students in reading, as well as to communicate to students that reading is valued by the school.

Some children will need assistance selecting books. Knowing students well—their interests and skill levels—enables teachers to make book recommendations. Other students will require support in using the allotted time to actually read. Although ideally the teacher reads along with the students, the teacher's most important responsibility is to ensure that all students read. This may mean that the teacher pulls aside individuals to read aloud very quietly to them, sits by students who are having difficulty staying focused, or conducts gentle but enthusiastic interviews of students regarding their books, expressing a sincere interest in what they are reading.

Teachers should also make efforts to have students read at other times during the school day and outside of school on a regular basis. They should talk to families at parent meetings, such as Back-to-School Night, about the importance of wide reading and assign free reading as homework. Our own children's teachers frequently required 30 minutes of reading for homework, with our signatures as documentation that the reading was completed. Although some teachers tell us that not all students will engage in assigned after-school reading unless there is greater accountability (e.g., completing a reading journal or book report), many students do read, and brief conversations with students the next morning about what they read may be just enough to nudge those who need more encouragement.

In addition to allotting time for reading at school and assigning after-school reading, teachers must express an interest in their students' reading by asking questions and making book recommendations based on their knowledge of the students' interests. This kind of teacher attention and encouragement can go a long way toward motivating students to read.

6. **Ensure Access and Choice**

In surveys and interviews, third- and fifth-grade students identified book access and book choice as two factors that positively influenced their motivation to read (Palmer, Codling, and Gambrell 1994). These factors, combined with similar findings by other researchers and our own experiences, lead us to urge teachers to make a variety of reading materials available in the classroom and to allow students to freely make their own reading selections.

Interestingly, Gambrell (1996) found that students overwhelmingly indicated that the classroom library was their primary source of books for independent reading—not the school library, not the public library, not their home libraries, but the classroom library. What does this mean for teachers? It means that if they want to develop avid readers, teachers must establish large classroom libraries that include a range of topics, text types, and levels to meet students' diverse interests and needs. Displaying books so they are easily viewed by the students and providing a comfortable environment for perusing and reading books are important components of a classroom library.

With a range of reading materials should come the opportunity for students to select what they want to read. Choice in the classroom is empowering. It communicates that students' interests are valued. Research documents that students are more inclined to read and enjoy reading if they are permitted to select their own reading materials on a regular basis.

7. **Engage Students in Social Interactions about Books**

If we want to motivate students to read, social interactions about books should be a regular part of the classroom program. Students should be provided with opportunities to talk about books they are reading and listen to classmates talk about their books. Opportunities can be formal, such as weekly small-group book shares for which the students prepare, or less formal, such as brief exchanges with a classmate after a sustained silent reading period. We believe that both types of experiences are important. Informal opportunities, however, should predominate, as they can be brief and frequent, be easily woven into the school day, and present students with many opportunities to hear about books from peers with whom they may not normally interact. Informal opportunities to share books include the following:

- Five minutes before recess, ask students to write on an index card or small piece of paper the name of a book they have recently read, heard someone read, or would like to read. Invite them to stand up, wander through the room with their cards, and share the names of the books and why they selected them with at least three other students. Students may want to exchange cards with the last student they talked to or with someone who shared a book that piqued their interest.

- After sustained silent reading time, tell the students to turn to a neighbor and share something about their books (or other reading material).

- After sustained silent reading time, ask one or two volunteers to share with the entire class something about the books they are reading.

- Conduct a quick survey around the room and have each student name the book he or she is currently reading. Students may also give a tentative rating of the book, indicating how much they like the book at this point in their reading.

Research confirms that social interactions involving books can be highly motivating in terms of influencing students to read (Palmer et al. 1994). Of course, this makes intuitive sense. Think for a moment about what motivates you to read. When we ask our adult students to name a book they recently read and share their reasons for selecting the book, statements such as the following are very common: "I chose it because my friend said it was a good book." "My sister read it and told me I should read it." "I heard some classmates talking about it and decided to pick it up." "My book club selected it." Peers can exert a powerful influence on individuals, and teachers can and should take advantage of that influence to motivate students to read.

# Reading Aloud to Students

Most teachers understand and appreciate the value of reading aloud to their students. Reading aloud promotes positive attitudes toward reading and supports literacy development by exposing students to text structures, building background knowledge, and sharing the rich language of books, including sophisticated vocabulary. Reading aloud is particularly important in classrooms of young children because these students are just learning to read and are not yet able to independently enjoy books that contain more challenging vocabulary. However, even older students benefit from hearing a good book read aloud.

Even as much as a single reading of a book has been found to contribute to the receptive vocabularies of young children. In a study by Sénéchal and Cornell (1993), students who listened to a storybook containing several words known to be unfamiliar to them were able to identify the meanings of the words after the book was read. Repeated readings of the same book facilitated both receptive and expressive vocabulary development; that is, students were able to identify the meanings of the new words and use the words on their own. Vocabulary growth was further enhanced when students were asked to respond to questions and encouraged to use the new words in their responses (Sénéchal 1997).

Indeed, the talk that surrounds a shared reading experience has been found to be beneficial for language development. Beck and McKeown (2001) summarized the research on students' active participation in read-alouds and identified several practices that are especially effective in supporting language growth. These practices include the following:

- Focus the discussion on major ideas in the book. (Teachers should promote talk that supports understanding of major text ideas rather than recall of discrete details.)

- Talk about ideas as they are encountered. (Waiting until the entire book has been read to talk about ideas appears to be less effective than encouraging talk about ideas as they appear in the book.)

- Provide students with opportunities to be reflective and participate in analytic talk. (Teachers should encourage students to reflect on ideas and respond to the book in analytical ways rather than accept quick, less thoughtful responses.)

Although little research has focused on the benefits of reading aloud in English to English language learners, experts asserted that reading aloud to students is important "because the teacher may be the only model of fluent reading and intonation patterns in English" (Dunlap and Weisman 2006, 94). One study found that providing explanations of new vocabulary during a read-aloud in English supported vocabulary growth among English language learners (Collins 2005). The researcher concluded that teachers of English language learners should not limit their students' opportunities to participate in read-aloud experiences. Even students with a minimum level of English proficiency can benefit from listening to books read aloud in English when unknown words are explained.

We hope that you read aloud in your classroom frequently and enthusiastically and that you engage your students in meaningful discussions about the books you read. Below, we describe four suggestions for promoting vocabulary growth through read-alouds.

# Strategies and Considerations for Reading Aloud

## 1. Text Talk

Text Talk was developed by Beck and McKeown (2001) as an approach to reading aloud that supports young students' comprehension and language development. As the teacher reads, he or she asks open-ended questions that require students to discuss text ideas. These questions focus on important information and are designed to elicit extended use of language. "What's going on?" "What do we know now?" "Why do you think…?" are all questions that require students to think about ideas in the text and provide more than single-word responses. Follow-up questions that ask for elaboration are often necessary, especially when teachers first use this strategy. Generic probes such as "What does that mean?" are effective follow-up questions, and repeating and rephrasing what the students said can also extend student talk. According to Beck and McKeown, questions that invite students to share background knowledge should be limited because too often, students share personal anecdotes that draw them away from the language and ideas of the text.

Contrary to more typical practice, in this strategy, the teacher shares the book's illustrations after the students have heard and talked about a portion of the book. Beck and McKeown noted that students often rely on pictures to gain information about a text and consequently pay less attention to the language of the book. Because one of the purposes of reading aloud is to expose children to the rich language of written text—to enable them to construct meaning from decontextualized language—showing illustrations before students have the chance to think about and talk about ideas conveyed by the words can be counterproductive.

Except in cases where the teacher thinks that knowledge of a word is needed for comprehension, discussion of words in the book occurs after the reading. This allows the book to provide a rich context for word learning. The teacher explains the meaning of a new word, asks the students to say the word, reminds the students of how the word was used in the story, and involves them in using the word in other contexts. In addition, students are encouraged to use the word over time. The teacher can post new words on a class chart, and students can tally each use of the word.

2. **Repeated Reading**

Some teachers are hesitant to read a book aloud more than once, yet young children often request favorite books again and again. The research cited earlier suggests that rereading is an effective practice, and this may be so for several reasons. Among them is that repeated reading provides students with greater familiarity with the information in the book and allows them to pay more attention to the special language of the book with each subsequent reading. For English language learners, repeated readings accompanied by comprehensible input, such as through pictures and gestures, can contribute to the acquisition of English (Dunlap and Weisman 2006).

Teachers of older students will not be likely to reread books they share aloud. Favorite read alouds such as O'Dell's *Island of the Blue Dolphins* (1960) or Curtis's *The Watsons Go to Birmingham—1963* (2001) are simply too long to read in their entirety more than once. However, rereading interesting portions of the books and making the books available to students to read independently provides students with repeated exposure to the powerful language in these books.

3. **Consider Text Level and Ensure Variety**

As we explained earlier in this chapter, in general, all types of written materials are better sources of new words than oral language experiences. However, we need to make two important points here. The first is that students learn new words most effectively from texts that are neither too easy nor too difficult. Therefore, as teachers select books to read aloud to students, one consideration should be the level of the books. Sharing books that are slightly above what the students are able to read or interact with on their own is essential if the goal is to promote vocabulary growth. Students have no opportunity to learn new words if the books contain only words that already exist in their vocabularies. Likewise, books that contain a great many words that are beyond the students' current word knowledge are likely to only frustrate students. Teachers must be thoughtful about selecting books at an appropriate level to share with their students.

Second, it is crucial that teachers read aloud a variety of types of books: narratives, poetry, informational books, biographies, and others. In particular, informational books have recently been emphasized as an essential component of literacy programs for a variety of reasons (Duke 2000; Spencer and Guillaume 2006; R. H. Yopp and Yopp 2000, 2006). One of the reasons is that they are outstanding sources of new words for students. As Scott (2005) explained, informational books are especially valuable for word learning because the words in informational books are often labels for important concepts and are therefore central to the overall meaning of the text. Further, word meanings are often explicitly or implicitly explained in informational books. In contrast, the descriptive words that are more typical of narrative texts are generally less essential to overall meaning and therefore more easily disregarded. Readers can skip over these words and still understand the text. To develop word knowledge, teachers should ensure that their read-aloud repertoires include a wide variety of text types, including informational books.

## 4. Share Engaging Books

In this era of text messaging, video games, and action movies, rich vocabulary is often nonexistent or takes a decidedly secondary role. If students are to develop powerful vocabularies and an appreciation for the importance of well-chosen words, then the nature of the literature that teachers introduce them to is of special importance. For example, reading aloud *Chicken Soup with Rice* (Sendak 1991), *Big Bad Bruce* (Peet 1977), or *Where the Red Fern Grows* (Rawls 1961) is a wonderful way to illustrate to students how the right words can make books a joy to read or to hear.

> "*I told you once, I told you twice, all seasons of the year are nice for eating chicken soup with rice.*" (*Chicken Soup with Rice* by Maurice Sendak, p. 25)

> "*Just then a raucous roar of laughter echoed through the pines, and in a twinkle Roxy caught sight of the bear on the bluff. 'So that's who!' she cried. And in a fury she went storming up the slope to face the bear.*" (*Big Bad Bruce* by Bill Peet, p. 11)

> "*As soon as his feet touched bottom in the shallow, he started bawling and lunging. White*

*sheets of water, knocked high in the moonlight by his churning feet, gleamed like thousands of tiny white stars." (Where the Red Fern Grows by Wilson Rawls, p. 74)*

Many award-winning books are filled with rich language. For vocabulary growth to occur, students need to encounter rare and wonderful words—words they may not encounter without teacher guidance. Ashton-Warner described how to teach students to read by stating, "First, words must mean something to a child" (1963, 33). Books that have received one or more of the following awards are almost always excellent choices to read aloud and will introduce students to rare, rich, and wonderful words—hopefully, words that will mean something to them.

- John Newbery Medal: The Newbery Medal honors the author of the most distinguished contribution to American literature for children each year.

- Randolph Caldecott Medal: The Caldecott Medal honors the artist of the most distinguished American picture book for children each year.

- Schneider Family Book Award: This award honors the author or illustrator of a book that portrays some aspect of the disability experience.

- Mildred L. Batchelder Award: The Batchelder Award is given to an American publisher of a children's book considered to be the most outstanding of those books originally published in a foreign country and subsequently translated into English and published in the United States.

- Pura Belpré Award: The Pura Belpré Award honors a Latino/Latina writer and illustrator who best portrays, affirms, and celebrates the Latino cultural experience in an outstanding work of literature for children and youth.

- Theodor Seuss Geisel Award: The Theodor Seuss Geisel Award honors the author(s) and illustrator(s) of the most distinguished contribution to the body of American children's literature known as *beginning reader books* published in the United States during the preceding year.

- Robert F. Siebert Informational Book Medal: The Robert F. Siebert Medal honors the author (including co-authors and author-illustrators) of the most distinguished informational book published during the preceding year.

- Laura Ingalls Wilder Award: The Laura Ingalls Wilder Award honors an author or illustrator whose books, published in the United States, have made, over a period of years, a substantial and lasting contribution to literature for children.

- Coretta Scott King Award: The Coretta Scott King Award honors African American illustrators and authors whose books promote an understanding and appreciation of the American dream.

Teachers need to ensure that multicultural books are among those read aloud. Hefflin and Barksdale-Ladd (2001) noted that personal connections with literature and positive attitudes toward reading are enhanced when students see themselves in books. Some of the award-winning books offer this opportunity. In addition, Dr. Rosario Ordoñez-Jasis, Ph.D., our colleague at California State University, Fullerton, recommends the following multicultural books for young listeners:

*Appalachia: The Voices of Sleeping Birds* by Cynthia Rylant (1998), illustrations by Barry Moser. This book utilizes rich language to describe the lives of those who live in Appalachia.

*Dumpling Soup* by Jama Kim Rattigan (2001), illustrations by Lillian Hsu-Flanders. This fictional book is about an Asian American girl living in Hawaii. As it tells a story about family traditions and making dumplings at New Year's, it incorporates the language and heritage of various Asian American and Hawaiian communities.

*Gathering the Sun* by Alma Flor Ada (1997), illustrations by Simon Silva. This alphabet book is richly illustrated by a very well-known artist and is written in both English and Spanish.

*Hairs/Pelitos* by Sandra Cisneros (1994), illustrations by Terry Ybáñez. This story, written in both English and Spanish, was taken from the popular book *The House on Mango Street*. It includes terrific descriptive words.

*Henry's Freedom Box: A True Story from the Underground Railroad* by Ellen Levine (2007), illustrations by Kadir Nelson. This wonderful book gives an account of how a slave mailed himself to freedom.

*The Invisible Thread* by Yoshiko Uchida (1991). This book gives an account of a young Japanese American girl, living in Berkeley, California during WWII, whose family is sent to an internment camp.

*Jalapeño Bagels* by Natasha Wing (1996), illustrations by Robert Casilla. This cute story is about a little boy growing up in a bicultural household and his efforts to navigate various worlds with a Mexican mother and a Jewish father.

*Thirteen Moons on Turtle's Back: A Native American Year of Moons* by Joseph Bruchac and Jonathan London (1992), illustrations by Thomas Locker. This book describes the seasons of the year through lovely poetry.

*Too Many Tamales* by Gary Soto (1992), illustrations by Ed Martinez. This book describes the customs, traditions, and family life of a Mexican American family during the holidays.

*South & North, East & West* collected by Michael Rosen (2007), various illustrators. This is a terrific collection of short stories from around the world (e.g., Brazil, Zimbabwe, China, Greece, the Middle East, and others).

# Conclusion

We began this chapter by asking you to think about your own independent reading and read-aloud practices. Do you read? What motivates you to read? Do you read aloud to your students? What does your reading aloud look like? These questions are important for every teacher who wishes to provide a rich vocabulary program for his or her students. It matters that you read. It matters that you think about what inspires you to read; children are not so different from adults! It also matters that you examine your read-aloud choices and practices and consider ways to enrich them.

In this chapter, we explained why written language is such an important source of new words and how it differs from oral language. We discussed two ways to expose students to written language—independent reading and reading aloud—and outlined several strategies and suggestions for engaging in these practices. If students are to add to their vocabularies, they need to encounter rare words—words not commonly found in high-utility word lists. It is clear from the research that there are huge differences among students in terms of reading volume and corresponding vocabulary growth. In schools everywhere, there are students who read very little, students who read a great deal but narrowly, and students who read widely and wisely. It is a teacher's special responsibility to guide students toward books that will both enrich their knowledge of the world and enhance their vocabularies. We hope our discussion bolstered an existing commitment to engage your students in wide reading and that the research and suggestions we shared provide you with new insights and ideas.

# Think About It!

1. Why is it important to move students beyond their immediate reading interests?

2. Explain why wide reading is beneficial to vocabulary growth.

3. What are three ways to motivate students to read widely?

4. Reflecting on your instructional setting, what are three topics around which you could build text sets that would be especially effective in promoting word learning?

# Chapter 4

# Establishing a Word-Conscious Environment

## Fun with Words!

Try to answer each of the following questions with pairs of rhyming words.

1. What do you call someone who is fascinated with language?

2. What do you call a movie about educators?

3. What do you call a learning institution that students enjoy attending?

4. What do you call the reaction to a good joke at a faculty meeting?

5. What do you call a child in your classroom who is cautious and uses good judgment?

6. What do you call a person who acts out words that sound alike?

## Answers

1. *A word nerd*

2. *A teacher feature*

3. *A cool school*

4. *A staff laugh*

5. *A prudent student*

6. *A rhyme mime*

> *"Whenever we come upon one of those intensely right words in a book or a newspaper the resulting effect is physical as well as spiritual."*
>
> —Mark Twain

Exposing students to rich oral and written language is crucial to their vocabulary development. Even more important is sparking their interest in and fascination with words. In fact, curiosity about words "is a hallmark of those who develop large vocabularies" (Beck, McKeown, and Kucan 2002, 13). Thus, an effective vocabulary program does more than expose students to words (Chapters 2 and 3) and provide them with instruction (Chapters 5 and 6); it stimulates word consciousness—an interest in learning words, learning about words, playing with words, and using words well.

Word consciousness includes both a cognitive stance and an affective stance toward words. Word-conscious students notice words, reflect on their own and others' word choices, and recognize the importance of making interesting choices. They appreciate words and are motivated to find just the right words to say what they want to say. They are intrigued by word histories and how language continues to evolve.

Teachers can and should build word consciousness throughout the school day and across the curriculum. In this chapter, we share a variety of strategies teachers can use to develop word consciousness in their students. The interest in words that teachers promote in their classrooms can last a lifetime and will support ongoing vocabulary development that extends beyond the classroom walls.

# Strategies for Creating Word Consciousness

The strategies we share are useful for stimulating students' interest in words, and they promote thinking and talking about words. They draw students' attention to words. They invite them to identify words they find interesting, important, or powerful. The strategies prompt them to explore and examine words. They engage students in wordplay, and they expose them to rich uses of words. These strategies reinforce and extend students' understanding of words they already know and introduce them to new words. Most of all, they help students appreciate words.

## 1. Word Walls

Many teachers incorporate word walls into their classrooms: They identify words that serve particular instructional purposes, record them on strips of tagboard or cardstock, and post them on a bulletin board, perhaps in alphabetical order. Sometimes the words are selected based on their frequency, such as when teachers are supporting students' learning of sight words. Sometimes they are selected based on their spelling, such as when teachers are supporting their students' awareness of spelling patterns or frequently misspelled words. Sometimes they are selected based on a topic of study, such as when teachers are supporting students' awareness and understanding of specialized content vocabulary. And sometimes they are selected for other purposes, such as because they are interesting or colorful or unusual. Often, teachers—and students—will add words to the walls over time. Most importantly, teachers will draw students' attention to the words by talking about them and inviting students to use them in their discussions and written work.

Word walls are useful means of raising students' word consciousness because they are part of the students' environment—one with which they interact—and they promote attention to and use of words. One classroom teacher we know asked his students to build a wall of words that could be used instead of the word *said*. Students' contributions included *remarked, stated, questioned, responded, shouted, whispered,* and *insisted,* to name only a few. The students referred to the wall regularly and soon *said* dropped out of their writing as they came to appreciate the nuances conveyed by the different words that appeared on the word wall.

Related to the word wall is the phrase wall. To enhance students' appreciation for the rich language used by authors, the teacher can ask students to periodically search their independent-reading books for a phrase that is interesting or powerful—one that captures the imagination or paints a picture. Students write the phrases on strips, record their names and the source of the phrases, including the page numbers, on the backs of the strips, and post them on the wall. Students can also select phrases they hear in songs, on television shows, or in conversations. Sources of language surround us! The teacher can later encourage the students to borrow phrases from the phrase wall and use them in their own writing.

2. **Words of the Week**

At the classroom level or the school level, teachers or students can select a word or two to highlight each week. With enthusiasm and fanfare, the words are introduced and explained at the beginning of the week, and then teachers and students challenge one another to use the words throughout the week—on the playground, in the lunch room, in the classroom, and in their homes.

At a local school, words are presented on the marquee in front of the school at the beginning of each week so family members who are dropping off their children are informed and can help students use the words at home. One week, for example, the word *symbol* was posted as the word of the week for the primary-grade students. The word *resilient* was posted as the upper-grade word. Everyone who drove past the school could see the words, and no doubt, many children provided examples of symbols to their parents or caregivers or explained what it means to be resilient and whether they are resilient as they drove home from school.

Throughout the week, the students' task was to use the word in their discussions and their writings, and each time an adult on campus heard or saw a student use the word, the student received a Good Word! card. Likewise, cards were given to students who were first to point out an adult's use of the word. Good Word! cards could be accumulated and traded in for various awards. The class with the most cards at the end of each day, for example, was first in the lunch line the following day. Students were enthusiastic about using the word and found many reasons throughout the school day to include the word in their oral and written language.

3. **Word Jars**

Inspired by the book *Donavan's Word Jar* by Monalisa DeGross (1998), this strategy involves depositing interesting words into a word jar. The book tells the story of a young boy who is just like his classmates in many ways. He is different, however, when it comes to collecting things. Donavan likes to collect words. He notices them in his environment, writes them on slips of paper, and drops them into a jar he keeps in his room.

After reading the book aloud to students, the teacher can suggest that the class start its own collection of words. The teacher can encourage students to notice words in conversations at school and at home, in books they are reading, and in their surroundings on their way to and from school. Words that appeal to them—that are new or interesting or sound good or roll around their mouths before sliding off their tongues—can be written on scraps of paper and dropped into the jar throughout the school day. The only rule is that students must find out what the words mean before they can put them into the jar. At the end of a given amount of time, perhaps a week, the students can dump the words onto a table, examine them, and talk about them. How do they sound? What do they mean? Where did we see or hear them? The students might vote on three words to serve as next week's words of the week. Or they might think of ways to use the words in sentences or sort the words. They might add them to a word wall or record the words they like in their personal dictionaries.

Students are often highly engaged by this strategy. They enjoy looking for words to add to the jar, and the level of enthusiasm increases as the jar fills. Generally, everyone wants to contribute at least one word. The astute teacher will notice those students who are not participating and provide support by helping them think about words in the books they are reading or words they are learning in various subject areas throughout the school day.

4. **Word Journals**

Word journals provide students with the opportunity to think about words in a story, a specialized content vocabulary word, or a word from any other source, and then identify one that is important to them. Students record the word in their daily word journals and share why it is important. The two sample entries below reveal students' understanding of the word as well as their efforts to make personal connections to the word.

*Expression—I picked the word* expression *because it was in the book we read today called* Officer Buckle and Gloria *by Peggy Rathmann (1995). In the book, students at Napville School are bored by the policeman's safety speech. Then his police dog partner, Gloria, joins him and acts out the safety hazards. Officer Buckle thinks the audience starts paying attention because he is using a lot of expression, but it's really because of Gloria. It is a funny book. I like it when people speak and read with expression, but I would like it more if a dog acted out safety rules!*

*Dribble*—Dribble *is a cool word. I like to dribble the ball in basketball, but I don't like it when milk dribbles out of my mouth. Today in P.E., we got to practice dribbling the ball. The word sounds funny, like it dribbles out of my mouth when I say it. That's why I picked it.*

This strategy encourages students to use new or interesting words in the context of a short paragraph. Some teachers ask students to write in a word journal every day and share their entries with classmates. Others collect the journals periodically and respond to students' words and ideas. At the end of a month, students can select their favorite words from their journals and share them with classmates or post them on a word wall. Student choice is powerful in stimulating interest, and sharing with peers increases motivation.

## 5. Preview-Predict-Confirm

Preview-Predict-Confirm (H. K. Yopp and Yopp 2006; R.H. Yopp and Yopp 2004) is a strategy that promotes thinking and talking about words as students use the rich context of text illustrations to generate topic-related words, categorize them, and identify several for sharing with the class. It is an easy strategy to implement, as it requires little preparation, yet it is a powerful strategy that actively engages students in conversations about words, their meanings, and the context in which the words are found. Furthermore, because the strategy draws on students' backgrounds, it honors diverse experiences and engages all learners.

The teacher begins by sharing the illustrations in a text— usually an informational text—and asking the students to anticipate the words the author may have used. Students offer suggestions, and the teacher asks them to share their reasoning. For example, third-grade students might respond to the illustrations in Jim Arnosky's *All About Owls* (1999) with the words *feathers, claws,* and *prey.* They might explain that one of the illustrations was a detailed drawing of the owl's body, including feathers and claws. They might also state that they saw pictures of an owl using its claws to grab a mouse and a rabbit, and that those animals are its prey. Another student might say *barn* because he or she knows some owls live in barns. After soliciting several word predictions and explanations from the class, the teacher organizes the students into groups of three or four and gives each group a set of 20 to 40 small pieces of cardstock or paper. Index cards cut into fourths are a good size. If the pieces are too large, they will be difficult to manipulate and view all at once.

In their small groups, the students generate words related to the topic of the text, basing their predictions on the illustrations and their own knowledge of owls. Groups record their words on the cards, one word per card, and should be challenged to use all of their cards. Students may need to be supported with questions such as the following:

- "What other pictures did you see?"

- "What else was in that picture?"

- "What could have been in the picture that perhaps the illustrator did not include?"

- "What do you know about owls?"

- "Have you ever seen an owl? Where? What was it doing?"

After providing the students with ample time to predict and record words, the teacher asks the students to sort the words in a way that makes sense to them and to label each group of words. In the case of the owl words, one group of students might sort words according to the following categories: body parts, environment, and things owls do. Additional blank cards should be made available at this time, as students often think of more words while sorting. The teacher then asks each group to quickly share its category labels (not the words) with the class. This sharing sparks further thinking about the words, and students may continue to add words.

Next the teacher asks each group of students to select three words for discussion with the class: a word they think every other group has (you might exclude the words that were shared with the class during the initial brainstorming), a word they think no other group has, and a word that interests them. The students record these three words on separate large cards so they can be seen by the entire class. A representative from each group stands in the front of the room to display the cards, first sharing the word the group thinks all groups will have. The teacher leads a discussion of the word choices, including what the words mean, how they are related to owls, and why they were selected. The same discussion occurs with the word each group thinks may be unique and then the interesting word.

Teachers find as they subsequently read the text that students are highly engaged with the material and eager to learn whether and how their word predictions appear in the text. The strategy heightens students' awareness of the words that make up the body of knowledge related to the topic. If you observe your students as they work in groups, you will find that they talk enthusiastically about words, clarify word meanings, and teach each other new words that are drawn from their experiences and background knowledge. Preview-Predict-Confirm also has obvious benefits for students in terms of their reading comprehension: It activates and builds background knowledge, helps students set purposes for reading, and stimulates active engagement with text.

### 6. Ten Important Words

Another strategy that draws students' attention to and encourages talk about words is Ten Important Words (H. K. Yopp and Yopp 2003). After introducing a text, the teacher asks the students to independently read it and identify 10 important words. Important words are those the students believe are key to understanding the information shared by the author. The students record their 10 words on sticky notes and when they are all finished, the teacher guides the students in building a class bar graph of the words by posting their words in columns on a piece of chart paper. Each column represents a different word, so if 20 students select the word *forty-niner* from a book about the California gold rush, 20 sticky notes, each with the word *forty-niner* on it, are stacked vertically in a single column of the bar graph. Different words appear in different columns.

The students examine the completed graph, and the teacher leads a discussion about the words: Which words were selected by the most students? What do these words mean? Why are they important? Which words were selected by fewer students? Why were they chosen? What do they mean, and how are they related to the topic? We find that students are curious about their classmates' choices and interested to see what the most selected words were. They likely will talk energetically about their decisions.

Next the students independently write a single-sentence summary of the reading selection and share it with a partner or small group. This sentence will often contain important words that were discussed by the class. Some teachers like to let students revise their Ten Important Word selections, write a brief explanation of their new choices, and submit them along with their summary sentences. Other teachers do not collect work from the students but carefully observe their participation in the strategy for purposes of assessment.

This strategy supports students' comprehension of a text while also drawing their attention to and reinforcing their understanding of words. Discussion of the words and their importance to a reading selection enhances students' knowledge of the word meanings and how the words are used. Most importantly, it heightens their attention to words used by the author, and because students have the opportunity to make personal choices about the importance of words, it strengthens their personal connection to the text.

Teachers can have students work in pairs if they believe that some students will find this strategy too challenging. Pairs can read the text aloud to each other and talk about and select their 10 important words together.

7. **Word Charts**

Word charts are completed in response to a reading. With this strategy, students respond to a brief portion of text with a word. In the case of narrative text, teachers can prompt students to generate a word that represents a character's feelings. For example, after reading or hearing the first several pages of *Ira Sleeps Over* by Bernard Waber (1972), approximately one-third of the students are asked to individually think of a word that describes how Ira feels, one-third are asked to think of a word that describes how his sister feels, and one-third are asked to think of a word that describes their own feelings at this point in the story. Students record their words on sticky notes and post them on a chart in the front of the room in the appropriate cell (e.g., "Ira," "His sister," "Me"). The teacher reads aloud all the word choices in the first cell of the chart and asks the students to share reasons for their selections. A student who wrote the word *concerned* might explain that Ira is concerned about going to a sleepover without his teddy bear. A student who selected *worried* might agree that Ira is thinking about how it might feel to be without his teddy bear and that he is worried about sleeping without it for the first time. The teacher and students talk about the meanings of the words and why they were selected. Then the teacher resumes reading, stops after another several pages, and asks the students to record and post new words to express how their characters feel, or how they themselves feel. Again, a discussion of the words follows.

This strategy offers the students a chance to think and talk about words and how they convey important information about characters, events, or concepts in a book. The focus on a single word heightens students' awareness of words, and after the first discussion, students often make an extra effort to carefully select words that they think their classmates will find interesting and meaningful.

The strategy may also be used with informational texts and class discussions, demonstrations, or other forms of instruction, including inductive approaches. The teacher stops periodically during a lesson (at times that he or she deems appropriate) and asks students to record a single word that somehow captures their understanding, thinking, or reactions to the content or experience up to that point. Students place their words on a chart, and the teacher, displaying enthusiasm for their words, leads a quick discussion before the lesson resumes. The content vocabulary remain on display, and the class revisits them as the subject continues to be explored.

## 8. Literature Circles

In Chapter 2, we discussed the value of having students meet in groups to discuss the content under study as a way to increase students' opportunities to talk and hear academic vocabulary. We described learning circles as an adaptation of Daniels' (1994) literature circles. Here we share the power of literature circles: small, temporary groupings of students who are reading the same book and meeting regularly to talk about what they have read.

Each student assumes a different role and therefore has something unique to contribute to the group conversation. Roles, which are rotated among the students, may include summarizer, questioner, connector, and illustrator. One vitally important role is that of a vocabulary enricher. The student with this role selects several words or phrases from the reading that he or she wishes to discuss with the group. The selections may be words or phrases he or she found intriguing, entertaining, unusual, important, or new. The vocabulary enricher shares his or her selections with the group, draws his or her groupmates back into the literature to explore how the author used the words, and shares his or her reasons for making these selections. By including this role in each literature circle, awareness of the author's language is heightened. Students talk about words, and their word consciousness is raised. Thinking about words becomes a habit.

## 9. Exploring Etymology

Etymology is the study of word origins. Thinking about how words originated can spark students' interest and delight in words. Consider the following:

- *Turncoat* refers, in modern usage, to someone who is disloyal. The word originated in medieval times when those working for or affiliated with a particular nobleman wore coats of the same color so they could be easily identified. In times of conflict, some people would literally turn their coats inside out in order to hide their association with the nobleman.

- The name of the fish *halibut* originated hundreds of years ago in England, where all flatfish were called "butts." There was one flatfish that was saved for eating on holy days. This fish was called the *haly* (holy) *butt*—the halibut.

- The *Frisbee* was named after the pie plates from the Frisbie Pie Company in Connecticut. Students near the factory used to throw the pie plates around to entertain themselves. The activity caught on and, in the 1950s, a plastic disk was manufactured in California and named for the pie company.

The origin of idioms can be equally fascinating, and sharing their histories may help students better understand their meanings. This may be particularly helpful for English language learners, who often experience difficulty with idioms. Here are a few examples of idioms and their origins:

- *Pulling my leg*: A common ploy of robbers in England years ago was to trip a passerby by stretching a wire or holding a cane across a walkway. When the unsuspecting passerby tripped and fell, he or she was robbed. The expression now means someone is trying to fool you.

- *Keep your shirt on*: Men often took off their shirts in order to fight because the shirts shrunk when washed and were too tight to permit easy movement of the arms. Taking off your shirt signaled that you were ready to throw a few punches. Encouraging someone to "keep his or her shirt on" is a way of telling the person to calm down.

- *To give someone the cold shoulder*: Dating back to medieval times, this idiom refers to the selection of meat offered to some castle visitors. Travelers who were offered hot meals knew they were welcome, but those offered a cold shoulder of mutton (i.e., sheep) understood that they were not welcome to stay.

Good sources of the origins of words include Funk and Funk's (1986) *Horsefeathers & Other Curious Words*, Ayto's (1990) *Dictionary of Word Origins: The Histories of More Than 8,000 English-Language Words*, and *The Merriam-Webster New Book of Word Histories* (1991).

Sometimes a word originates from a combination of two words, someone's name, a location, or another language. Here we share portmanteaux, eponyms, toponyms, and words borrowed from other languages.

## Portmanteaux

*Portmanteaux* are words that are formed by combining the sounds and meanings of two or more words. Sometimes called "blends," portmanteaux are coined to capture new ideas. For instance, *smog* is a portmanteau for smoke and fog. A popular game has a portmanteau as a name: *Pictionary*® (from picture + dictionary). The father of two of the authors was the director of *Avionics* (aviation + electronics) at an aircraft company for many years. A fast-food place we frequent provides rounded spoons with forked edges that are referred to as *sporks* (spoon + fork). One of the author's daughters and her girlfriends use portmanteaux such as *ginormous* (gigantic + enormous) and *fantabulous* (fantastic + fabulous) regularly. Some portmanteaux, such as *fortnight* (fourteen + nights), have been a part of the English language for hundreds of years, while others, such as *netiquette* (Internet + etiquette), are very new additions to the language.

A few additional portmanteaux you might recognize include the following:

- breakfast + lunch = *brunch*

- motor + hotel = *motel*

- television + evangelist = *televangelist*

- simultaneous + broadcast = *simulcast*

- web + log = *blog*

- condensation + trail = *contrail*

- parachute + troop = *paratroop*

- chuckle + snort = *chortle*

- free + software = *freeware*

- partner + alimony = *palimony*

- biology + electronic = *bionic*

## Eponyms

Eponyms are words that are derived from the name of a person. The name *America* came from the explorer Amerigo Vespucci. Several of the United States were named after important figures. For example, Virginia and West Virginia were named in honor of Queen Elizabeth I, the Virgin Queen; *Georgia* in honor of George II; the *Carolinas* in honor of Charles I; and *Maryland* in honor of Henrietta Maria, wife of Charles I. *Louisiana* was named in honor of Louis XIV of France. *Pennsylvania* took its name from Sir William Penn, father of the founder of the state, and *Washington* was named for George Washington.

Words that your students might not have realized were named after people include the following. Many more can be found by searching *eponyms* on the Internet.

- *boycott*: named after Charles C. Boycott, a nineteenth-century English landlord who was ostracized for refusing to reduce rents

- *braille*: named after Louis Braille, a French teacher of the blind

- *caesarean*: named after Julius Caesar, who is believed to have been delivered this way

- *Doberman*: named after a German dog catcher and police officer, Karl Friedrich Louis Dobermann, whose years of selective breeding of dogs produced the breed

- *Ferris wheel*: named after its inventor, George Washington Gale Ferris

- *Granny Smith apple*: named after Maria Ann Smith, an Australian woman who discovered this variety of apple in her orchard in the 1800s

- *guillotine:* named after the French physician, J. I. Guillotin, who pled for a swift form of execution during the French Revolution

- *sandwich*: named after John Montagu, 4th Earl of Sandwich, who, in order to play cards while eating, was served meat between two slices of bread

- *sideburns*: named after Civil War General Ambrose Burnside, who was known for prominent whiskers

## Toponyms

Toponyms are words that are named after a place. For instance, *bikini* derived its name from Bikini Atoll, where the first atom bomb was dropped, because it was thought that the bathing suit would have an explosive effect. The *duffel* bag got its name from the Belgium town of Duffel, where the woolen cloth was first made. Also originating from the name of a Belgium town is the word *spa*, a place of healing waters. *Hamburger,* which contains ground steak, not ham, was also named after its place of origin: Hamburg, Germany.

## Words from Other Languages

English has historically been a very welcoming language. Words from other languages are readily embraced and absorbed in the ever-expanding English language. We've included a small sampling of familiar words borrowed from other languages.

- Spanish: *alligator, avocado, chocolate, mosquito, canyon, guitar, lunch, ranch, rodeo, tuna, patio*

- French: *antique, ballet, beige, biscuit, cache, camouflage, chauffeur, coupon, debris, detour, grape, menu, niece, restaurant, rouge, saucer, soup, unique*

- German: *kindergarten, dollar, luck, muffin, nickel, pretzel, waltz, yodel, Fahrenheit*

- Italian: *opera, umbrella, macaroni, pizza, piano, spaghetti, trio, violin, volcano*

- Danish: *fog, kidnap, smile*

- Dutch: *ballast, amidships, cackle, easel, elope, trawl, waffle*

- Farsi: *bazaar, caravan, checkmate, lemon, pistachio, pajama, spinach, tiger*

- Arabic: *caramel, algebra, coffee, cork, cotton, garbage, giraffe, jar, mirror, monkey, safari, syrup, zero, admiral, artichoke*

- Japanese: *judo, karate, karaoke, futon, origami*

- Portuguese: *breeze, embarrass, cobra, flamingo, molasses, marmalade*

**English Continues to Grow**

Words continue to be added to the English language. Some new words added to a recent edition of the *Concise Oxford English Dictionary* (Revised Eleventh Edition) (www.askoxford.com/worldofwords/newwords/?view=uk) include the following:

- *shoulder-surfing*: the practice of spying on the user of a cash-dispensing machine in order to gain personal information

- *tri-band*: having three frequencies (referring to a mobile phone), thus allowing use in different regions of the world

- *upskill*: to teach an employee new skills

## 10. Special Words and Wordplay

When students have fun with and manipulate words to amuse, create a certain effect, or have an impact on others, they begin to more closely attend to words. The following word uses or riddles increase students' awareness of the words in our language.

- *Onomatopoeia* refers to words that sound like their meanings. *Buzz, bang, gulp, hiss, whirr,* and *kerplunk* all imitate the sounds they represent. Students can search for these words or create some of their own. Students who speak more than one language can share examples from other languages.

- *Hink Pinks* are riddles that have as an answer two one-syllable words that rhyme. For instance, what do you call an angry father? A mad dad. What do you call a boy who is crying? A sad lad. Hinky pinkys have two-syllable rhyming words for answers. What do you call an amusing rabbit? A funny bunny. Hinkity pinkitys have three-syllable rhyming words as answers. What is the White House? The president's residence. Students can develop riddles to share with one another. How did you do on the Hink Pinks and Hinky Pinkys at the beginning of this chapter?

- *Alliteration* refers to a phrase or sentence in which most of the words start with the same sound. When students are asked to use alliteration, they attend closely to words, think carefully about word choices, and begin to notice alliteration in their environment. They might see *William's Warehouse, Houston Hotel,* and *Sam's Software Sale* in their community. Alliteration is used in some book titles, such as *Maniac Magee* (Spinelli 1990), *Missing May* (Rylant 2004), *Lilly's Purple Plastic Purse* (Henkes 1996), *Beautiful Blackbird* (Bryan 2003), *Pride and Prejudice* (Austin, 1813), and *Of Mice and Men* (Steinbeck, 1937).

Teachers might ask students to examine poems to find alliteration and then write their own poetry using alliteration.

- When a person's name seems particularly well suited for his or her work, the name is an *aptronym*. Some examples of aptronyms are Mrs. Learn, a teacher; Mr. Wheel, a truck driver; Dr. Well, a physician, and Ms. Whistle, a train conductor. Students can be encouraged to develop their own lists of aptronyms or to use aptronyms in their writing.

- Students can also create *Tom Swifties*, which are quotations accompanied by a word that has a semantic relationship with the quote. For instance, "Slow down," drawled Akina; "I need to sharpen my pencil," Rochelle said pointedly.

## 11. Games

Teachers should not miss out on opportunities to make available in their classrooms the many entertaining and educational games that focus on words. Games such as Upwords®, Balderdash®, Boggle®, Password®, Scrabble®, Scattergories®, Pictionary®, Cranium®, and Syzygy® stimulate an interest in words, reinforce vocabulary knowledge, and introduce students to new vocabulary. Games may be played during a designated game time, on occasions when students remain indoors during recess and lunch due to inclement weather, or during special after-school events. Students can even bring their own games in from home and teach their peers how to play. Once students learn, they likely will request the opportunity to play again. Even better, they may encourage their families to purchase the games so they can play at home, where the fun with words continues! Teachers may wish to pair English language learners with more proficient peers to ensure they are included in the games and experience success.

## 12. Technology

Wordplay extends beyond the classroom to the Internet. Three of our favorite websites that offer interesting information about words, word games, and lessons are the following:

- **www.factmonster.com**—Fact Monster has a section called "Word Wise," which offers interesting language facts, information on idioms and proverbs, commonly used foreign words and phrases, and more.

- **www.m-w.com**—This is the Merriam-Webster dictionary site. It contains interesting information about word origins and also has word games.

- **www.readwritethink.org**—Sponsored by the International Reading Association in collaboration with the National Council of Teachers of English, this site provides educators with lessons on language arts topics, including vocabulary.

## 13. Share Children's Literature

Many delightful trade books play with or draw attention to words. One of our favorites is *Frindle* by Andrew Clements (1996). It is the story of a fifth-grade boy who invents a new word, much to the apparent dismay of his language arts teacher, the dictionary-loving Mrs. Granger. Many books, at a range of reading levels, draw attention to words. We hope teachers read them aloud, talk about them, and make them available to students. Students may then wish to author their own books that highlight words. We offer a brief list of books here:

- Amato, Mary. *The Word Eater*. New York: Holiday House, 2000.

- Clements, Andrew. *Frindle*. New York: Simon & Schuster, 1996.

- Falwell, Cathryn. *Word Wizard*. New York: Clarion Books, 1998.

- Frasier, Debra. *Miss Alaineus: A Vocabulary Disaster*. San Diego, CA: Harcourt Brace, 2000.

- Gwynne, Fred. *A Chocolate Moose for Dinner*. New York: Simon & Schuster, 1989.

- Gwynne, Fred. *The King Who Rained*. New York: Aladdin, 2006.

- Gwynne, Fred. *A Little Pigeon Toad*. New York: Simon & Schuster, 1988.

- Gwynne, Fred. *The Sixteen Hand Horse*. New York: Prentice Hall Books, 1980.

- Heller, Ruth. *Kites Sail High: A Book About Verbs*. New York: Putnam & Grosset Group, 1988.

- Heller, Ruth. *Many Luscious Lollipops: A Book About Adjectives*. New York: Putnam & Grosset Group, 1989

- Heller, Ruth. *Merry-Go-Round: A Book About Nouns*. New York: Putnam & Grosset Group, 1998.

- Heller, Ruth. *Up, Up and Away: A Book About Adverbs*. New York: Grosset & Dunlap, 1991.

- Hughes, Shirley. *Over the Moon: A Book of Sayings*. London: Faber and Faber, 1980.

- Juster, Norton. *As: A Surfeit of Similes*. New York: Morrow, 1989.

- Maestro, Betsy, and Giulio Maestro. *All Aboard Overnight: A Book of Compound Words*. New York: Clarion Books, 1992.

- Parish, Peggy. *Amelia Bedelia*. New York: Harper & Row, 1963.

- Parish, Peggy. *Thank You, Amelia Bedelia*. New York: HarperCollins, 1964.

- Presson, Leslie. *What in the World Is a Homophone?* Hauppauge, NY: Barron's, 1996.

- Sanvoisin, Eric. *Ink Drinker*. New York: Random House, 2008.

- Schwartz, David. *If You Hopped Like a Frog*. New York: Scholastic, 1999.

- Snicket, Lemony. *The Bad Beginning. (A Series of Unfortunate Events.)* New York: HarperCollins, 1999.

- Terban, Marvin. *Eight Ate: A Feat of Homonym Riddles*. New York: Clarion Books, 1982.

- Terban, Marvin. *Guppies in Tuxedos: Funny Eponyms*. New York: Clarion Books, 1988.

- Terban, Marvin. *In a Pickle and Other Funny Idioms*. New York: Clarion Books, 1983.

- Terban, Marvin. *Mad as a Wet Hen! And Other Funny Idioms*. New York: Clarion Books, 1987.

- Terban, Marvin. *Superdupers! Really Funny Real Words*. New York: Clarion Books, 1989.

- Terban, Marvin. *Your Foot's on My Feet! And Other Tricky Nouns*. New York: Clarion Books, 1986.

- Walton, Rick. *Once There Was a Bull…(Frog)*. New York: Putnam & Grosset Group, 1998.

# Conclusion

If teachers wish to promote ongoing vocabulary development, it must be a goal to turn all students into *logophiles*—lovers of words. Teachers can create conditions in their classrooms that stimulate students' desire to learn words and use them creatively and powerfully. By establishing a word-conscious environment across the curriculum, teachers contribute to students' willingness to embrace new words, actively seek out new words, and keep their eyes, ears, hearts, and minds wide open for appealing and interesting words.

# Think About It!

1. What word games do you enjoy? How do you share them with your students? How do you incorporate them into your school day?

2. Think about a recent time when you drew your students' attention to a word. How did you do so? What was your reason for doing so? Did your students respond with interest? How do you model an enthusiasm for words?

3. Anthroponomastics is the study of anthroponyms (Gk. Anthropos, "man," + onuma, "name"), the names of human beings. In investigating our own names, we found the following: *Ashley* is of Old English origin and means "dweller in an ash grove." In its early history, it was primarily a boy's name, but in recent years has become a popular girl's name. *Hallie* is most likely of Greek origin and means "thinking of the sea." *Ruth* is of Hebrew origin and means "friend" or "companion." Learn about the origin of your name.

# Chapter 5

# Teaching Words

## Knowledge Ratings

Using the scales below, please rate your current understanding of each term.

"Tier Two words" _____

"friendly explanation" _____

"word maps" _____

"content links" _____

1. Never heard it

2. Heard it; no idea what it means

3. Have some idea of what it means

4. Have a pretty good idea of what it means

5. Know it well and use it

*"One's vocabulary needs constant fertilizing..."*

—Evelyn Waugh

We noted in Chapter 1 that good teachers do not rely solely on incidental learning—the learning that occurs through oral language experiences, wide reading, and in word-conscious environments—to develop students' vocabularies. They also thoughtfully and deliberately select words to teach their students and plan instructional experiences that ensure active engagement with words as well as multiple exposures to them in rich contexts. We begin this chapter with a brief discussion of selecting words for study. Then we describe a number of strategies for teaching selected words and engaging students in thinking about, talking about, and using those words.

## Selecting Words to Teach

Not all words call for instructional attention. Indeed, there are some words that students already know, and there are others that they have little need to know at the present time ... or possibly ever! Further, as we noted in Chapter 1, there is not enough time in the 13-plus years of pre-K through 12th grade schooling to teach all the words that constitute the English language. The difficult task faced by the teacher, then, is how to determine which words to target for instruction. Fortunately, several literacy experts have shared perspectives that will be helpful when making that decision.

Beck, McKeown, and Kucan (2002), for example, described three tiers of words in a vocabulary. The first tier of words consists of the most basic words in a language. These Tier One words are high-frequency words that many students—except perhaps English language learners or students with special needs—are likely to already know. *Desk, pencil,* and *run* are examples. These words generally do not need to be taught and thus are not good candidates for instruction. At the other end of the spectrum are Tier Three words. Tier Three words are low-frequency words that may be limited to specific domains and do not have broad application for students. Tier Three words might include *polymerization*, *harrow*, and *impressment*. Note that these words are unlikely to be encountered by students other than in the context of specific content instruction. Because the words have limited general usefulness, it has been suggested that they should be taught only when the specific need arises.

It is the words between these levels—Tier Two words—that Beck et al. believe teachers should target for instruction. Tier Two words are not so basic that students already know them and are of high-enough frequency that students are likely to read them multiple times and in multiple contexts. Beck et al. shared the following examples: *coincidence*, *absurd*, *industrious*, and *fortunate*.

Because teachers often select words for instruction from an assigned reading, such as a work of literature or a textbook chapter, Beck and her colleagues suggest that teachers develop word lists by first previewing the text and identifying terms that are likely to be unfamiliar to many of the students and then editing the list to include only those words that are key to understanding the selection and have broad usefulness. The word *entablature*, used to describe a feature of a character's castle-like home, for example, might be identified as an unfamiliar word but eliminated from the list. The teacher will likely briefly explain the word to help students appreciate the setting of the story, but decide that the word is not worthy of valuable instructional time because of its limited future usefulness. Conversely, the teacher may add words to a list. If there are only a few words in the reading that warrant instruction, the teacher may use this as an opportunity to introduce words that are related in meaning to words in the selection. For example, if an author describes a character as *happy* when he or she receives good news, the teacher might include *elated* and *jubilant* on the vocabulary list.

Discussing vocabulary choices with colleagues whose students are reading the same text can be helpful to teachers who are generating word lists. Keep in mind, however, that identifying Tier Two words is not an exact science, and so it is reasonable to expect lists to differ. The insights provided by colleagues, however, and the opportunity to share your thinking about word selections can be beneficial.

Marzano (2004) shared a different perspective about which words to choose for instruction. In fact, he stated that selecting Tier Two words is a mistake and suggested that word frequency should not guide teachers' decisions. Instead, he advocated for targeting subject-specific terms, or what Beck et al. would consider Tier Three words, arguing that words that develop students' academic vocabulary and background knowledge will be more beneficial to their school success. Marzano provided a list of 7,923 subject-specific terms across 11 academic content areas for teachers to target for instruction.

Hiebert (2005) recommended that a vocabulary curriculum be both "effective" and "efficient." An effective vocabulary curriculum is one that focuses on words that are both unfamiliar to students and account for a significant portion of the words students will encounter in future readings (similar to Tier Two words). An "efficient" curriculum is one in which students have opportunities for multiple exposures to the words, such as through the study of words that have the same root (e.g., *satisfy* and *satisfaction*). Learning words from the same semantic families supports learning of other related words. Hiebert also advocated for the inclusion of specialized content-area words in a school vocabulary curriculum.

We believe that each of these perspectives has value. Teaching students words that they do not already know and are likely to encounter again in many contexts, specialized content vocabulary words, and words that have generative power are all vital components of a vocabulary curriculum. Teachers must thoughtfully incorporate the study of vocabulary into all areas of the curriculum, targeting words students are likely to encounter again, words that build their academic vocabularies and knowledge, and words that will support their understanding of related words.

# Strategies for Teaching Words

In this section, we provide strategies for teaching words. Recall that various authorities, including the National Reading Panel (NICHD 2000), emphasize that vocabulary instruction should involve:

- learning words in rich contexts

- repeated exposure and multiple opportunities to use new words

- exploring relationships among words

- active engagement with words on the part of the students

- a variety of practices

Each of the strategies we share is based on these principles of effective vocabulary instruction. We organize our presentation of the strategies according to their primary purpose and when they are likely to occur instructionally. First we share three strategies that are intended to spark students' curiosity about words and provide the teacher with the opportunity to assess what the students already know about the words and the concepts they represent. Then we describe strategies for introducing new words to students, followed by strategies for reinforcing and extending students' understanding of words. Finally, we discuss strategies that require students to use words in related or new contexts. Of course, we hope that teachers will be flexible in their use of these strategies and will find opportunities and reasons to utilize them for purposes and in ways other than those described here.

# Before You Teach

## 1. Knowledge Ratings

Teachers use a variety of methods to determine what students already know—or think they know—about a word or concept before teaching. One of our favorites is a strategy called Knowledge Ratings. With this strategy, teachers ask the students to rate their understanding of a word or words, much in the same way that we asked you to rate your knowledge of the terms at the beginning of this chapter. Teachers can use rating scales, as we did, and ask students to place a mark along a scale ranging from "never heard it" to "use it and know it well" for each word. Or teachers can ask students to identify whether they have certain types of knowledge about a word. Fisher and Blachowicz (2007), for example, suggest that students indicate whether they know a category or synonym for a word and can identify some characteristics that distinguish the word from others in the same category. Teachers can collect the students' responses, review them, and determine how much the students think they know about a word or words prior to teaching them. They can identify which students have a deep understanding of the word and which have no knowledge of the word.

Other formats for eliciting information about students' word knowledge include the following:

- Printed Targets (concentric circles): Students place a mark on a target to indicate their level of knowledge of a word—the closer to the center circle, or bull's-eye, the more the student thinks he or she knows and the more experience he or she has had with the word (Guillaume, Yopp, and Yopp 2007). The teacher might provide a small target for each word, just as we provided a scale for each word at the beginning of this chapter. The student places an *x* in the appropriate location on each target. Or the teacher might provide each student with one larger target and a short list of words. The students record the words on the target at locations representing their level of knowledge, perhaps writing some words in the bull's-eye and others in the outer rings of the target. Figure 5.1 shares one student's target for three words the teacher selected from the book *Chrysanthemum* by Kevin Henkes (1996).

**FIGURE 5.1 Knowledge rating target**

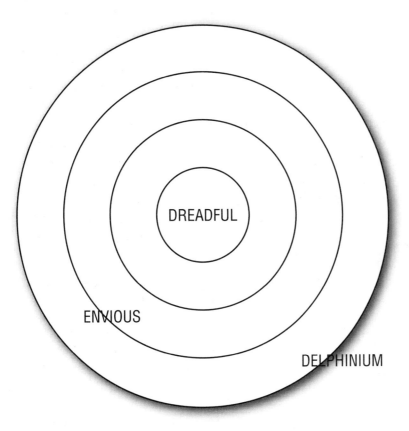

- Colored Dots: Students read words listed on a piece of paper and place a green dot sticker or draw a green dot (i.e., "go ahead—I know this") next to each word they know well, a yellow dot (i.e., "slow down and review") next to each word they have heard and for which they have a general sense of the meaning, and a red dot (i.e., "stop and teach me") next to each word they have never heard or know very little about.

- Various Sizes of Paper: The teacher provides students with varying sizes of pieces of paper, such as a full sheet of lined paper, a half sheet of paper, an index card, and a sticky note. Students reflect on how much they know about a word presented by the teacher by considering how much they are able to say about it. If they could fill a page with what they know, they hold up the full sheet. If they know less, they hold up an appropriately sized sheet.

In addition to providing individual response sheets or signals for students to use to indicate their degree of knowledge about words, the teacher can ask students to indicate their ratings on a group chart. Group charts provide information about the class at a glance and should be completed anonymously so students who do not feel comfortable sharing how much they know or do not know do not have to publicly declare their ratings. One strategy is to ask students to place an $x$ on a class scale or target (or a dot on a chart) posted near the door as they walk out of the room at the end of a class period or day. Or, students could be asked to find time during the day to contribute their ratings to the group chart.

After school, the teacher can quickly assess the students' depth of knowledge about the words. If most students indicated little knowledge of a word, the teacher might conclude that more or different instruction would be required than if most students indicated extensive knowledge. Additionally, the teacher learns that students may not be able to support classmates' understanding of a concept because most have limited understanding themselves. If there is a range of responses, the teacher learns that some students may have a great deal of understanding, while others may know little; therefore, some students may serve as valuable resources for others. Information about student knowledge will influence the teacher's instructional decisions, including those related to how much background information he or she provides, how much time he or she spends on the term, how he or she organizes for instruction, how he or she uses discipline-related language, and how he or she utilizes visuals and real-world examples.

Knowledge ratings are a quick and easy way to gain a general sense of students' comfort levels with a word. Of course, students' ratings are not always accurate and sometimes students who think they know a word well actually know very little. Sagacious teachers use multiple sources of information to make instructional decisions. Knowledge ratings do, however, provide the teacher with important information about what the students think they know or do not know.

Additionally, we have found that completing these ratings prompts students to ask questions and start talking with one another about words and their meanings. The curiosity and conversations sparked by this strategy support a level of engagement with the lesson that is beneficial to student learning.

Knowledge ratings can be used again after instruction, giving the teacher and the students an appreciation for what they have learned—and perhaps still need to know—about words and the concepts they represent in a unit of study.

2. **Possible Sentences**

Possible Sentences (Stahl 1999) is a strategy that requires students to think about a small number of words and how they are related to one another. Several versions have been described in the literature. In our version, the teacher identifies two or three words from a reading selection or upcoming lesson that he or she thinks the students may not know, along with a word or two that the teacher suspects the students do know. The words are listed on a chart or the board and pronounced for the students. The students are asked to say them, and then students individually (or in partners) generate a single sentence containing all the words. The teacher should explain that the students probably don't know all the words, but they should make good guesses as to what the words might mean and how they might be used. Students think about whether and where they have encountered these words before, how they might be related to the reading or unit of study, and how the words might be connected to each other. After the students have been given a few minutes to generate and record their sentences, they share their sentences with partners or in small groups, and then volunteers read their sentences to the entire class.

The teacher comments with interest on the various interpretations of the words and the connections students made among them, taking note of the students' level of knowledge. The teacher asks for additional thoughts from the students and then shares the reading selection or lesson. Students' attention to the words is usually heightened, and they construct and refine their understanding of the words as they engage in the reading or lesson activities. At the conclusion of instruction, the students share what they have learned about the words and may be asked to reject or revise their original sentences based on new understandings or to compose new sentences that contain the words.

The selected words are not usually found in a single sentence in the reading or lesson, but asking students to use them together in one sentence compels them to think about the relationships among the words and provides the teacher with information about what the students know. Possible Sentences is a useful tool for determining students' depth of understanding about words they are soon to encounter.

One fifth-grade group was given the words *crucible*, *apprentice*, *proportion*, and *silversmith* before reading a chapter in *Johnny Tremain* (Forbes 1945), a story set in Boston during the American Revolution. The sample sentences shared below provided the teacher with insight into her students' varied levels of knowledge about the words. What do they tell you about the students' understanding of the words?

> *The silversmith told his apprentice to use correct proportions when he added material to the crucible.*

> *The silversmith and crucible did not proportion the apprentice.*

> *The apprentice and the silversmith used the crucible to proportion.*

3. **Known and New Chart**

This strategy is useful for motivating students to learn new words and for assessing what students already know about the specialized vocabulary of a content area. Similar to Ogle's (1986) K-W-L (Know, Want to Know, Learned) strategy, the teacher begins the lesson or unit by asking students to brainstorm what they already know about the topic to be studied. Instead of asking the students to record ideas, however, the teacher asks them to list words. In a study of magnets, for example, the students individually or in small groups generate lists of words, such as *attract*, *repel, magnetism, pole*, and *compass*. Then they share their lists with the class, and the teacher records them in the "Known" column of a two-column class chart. The teacher invites the students to talk with partners about what they think they know about the meanings of the listed words.

Throughout the unit of study, the students identify topic-related words to be recorded in the "New" column of the chart. The teacher records the words they share, or he or she leaves the chart accessible to the students, and they periodically record words as they encounter them. In our magnets chart, they might record *force, bar magnet, horseshoe magnet, electromagnet, nickel,* and *iron,* for example. The teacher uses a variety of strategies, such as those shared in the next section of this chapter, to support student learning of these words.

The chart remains posted in the room throughout the unit of study so students can refer to the vocabulary words when they talk and write about the subject matter.

## Introducing Words

### 1. Friendly Explanations

Many authorities—and our own experiences—suggest that dictionary definitions are not very helpful for many students. In fact, researchers have found that when students are asked to construct sentences using words they have looked up in the dictionary, they often write sentences judged to be odd (Miller and Gildea 1985) or unacceptable (McKeown 1993). Instead of asking students to obtain definitions from dictionaries, teachers should provide "student-friendly explanations" of the words (Beck et al. 2002). Student-friendly explanations use familiar terminology to explain the meanings of the words, as well as provide examples of how the words might be used and by whom. Using everyday language, teachers share word meanings and contextual information, including, if appropriate, nuances or connotations that make it clear how a word might be used.

Recently, one of the authors' spouses, Tom, used the term *ice pick* in a conversation and was promptly asked by a child in the room what an ice pick is. It was interesting to listen to his response. Contrast what he said to the dictionary definition.

Tom: "An ice pick is a hand tool that is used to break ice. It is usually about this long (indicating about 10 inches), has a wooden handle, and a thin, sharp, steel point. People strike ice with the pick to break it into smaller chunks (grasping an imaginary ice pick and gesturing). Ice picks used to be very common. People needed ice picks in order to break up blocks of ice they bought—cubes and crushed ice weren't available—and put the pieces into their iceboxes to keep food cool. This was before refrigerators were invented. Ice picks are not very common anymore, but some people still have them. They can be dangerous, so you must be careful if you use one!"

Dictionary: "tool for breaking ice" (*DK Dictionary* 1997, p. 208)

Note that Tom's response used familiar language and provided sufficient detail so the boy could get a mental picture of the tool, understand its purpose, and gain a sense of its historical role in food preservation. Later, Tom explained the word *ultimatum.*

Tom: "An ultimatum is a final choice. You are telling the person, 'You either do this or something will happen.' Often, it's a threat, like, 'You either make your bed or you will spend the day in your room!' *Ultimate* means 'final'; *ultimatum* means 'final offer.'"

Dictionary: "final demand, terms offered by person of power" (*DK Dictionary* 1997, p. 475)

Teachers who want students to gain an accurate understanding of a word take the time to discuss the word and share examples of its use. They provide explanations of words similar to those provided by Tom. A friendly explanation can be followed by a review of a dictionary definition, if the teacher chooses. Dictionary skills are important, and dictionary definitions can support student understanding of a word. However, the unfortunately all-too-common strategy of asking students to look up words in a dictionary and write sentences using the words is not very effective.

2. **Semantic Maps**

Semantic Maps are graphic organizers that display the knowledge associated with a concept. They may be used to teach students new words or to review words already introduced. Dan, one of the authors' sons, recently joined the golf team at his high school. In a very short time, he encountered a new set of vocabulary words, including *birdie, bogey, double bogey, par, course, hole, fairway, green, tee, rough, sand trap, lateral, woods, irons, wedges, driver, putter, match, drive, putt,* and *chip*. The coach explained what the terms meant as they were used, and he and the experienced members of the team used the words repeatedly in context. Soon, Dan was very comfortable with the words. However, his mother often had difficulty understanding what he was talking about when he came home from practice. Finally, she asked him to help her understand the words by developing a semantic map. She needed to visualize how the terms were related to one another. Figure 5.2 shows what he drew. Later, he added lines that connected the different types of clubs with the areas of the course on which they are used. For example, he drew a line from *putters* to *green* and from *wedges* to *sand trap* and *rough*.

**FIGURE 5.2  Semantic Map for *golf***

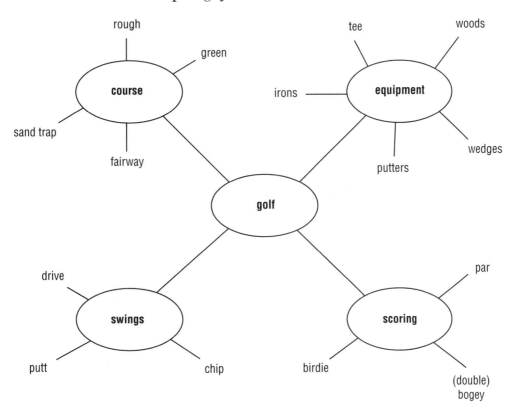

Along with his friendly definitions and demonstrations with his equipment, this graphic went a long way in helping his mother learn the words so she could engage in conversations about the sport with her son.

Teachers can introduce new vocabulary to students by drawing semantic maps on the board or chart paper, talking about the maps, and keeping them on display for students' reference. Often, students will be able to contribute to the maps by providing categories or examples related to the main concept. We observed a second-grade teacher use this strategy to introduce the concept of metamorphosis to her young students one morning. She wrote the word on the board, pronounced it for the students, and indicated that the students would soon be reading *Monarch Butterfly* by Gail Gibbons (1989). She asked the students to share what they knew about butterflies, and soon one of the students said that butterflies "come from caterpillars." She explained that the change that caterpillars undergo when they transform into butterflies is called a *metamorphosis*. She drew a circle around the word and then developed the categories depicted in figure 5.3. Students helped her generate the information that is displayed in the map below.

**FIGURE 5.3 Semantic Map for *metamorphosis***

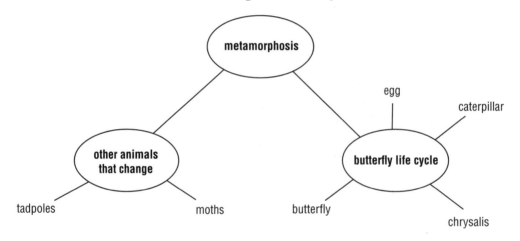

An important aspect of semantic mapping is the talk that accompanies it (Blachowicz et al. 2006). Students should be prompted to verbalize the relationships that are displayed on the map and talk about the information.

3. **Frayer Model**

The Frayer Model (Frayer, Frederick, and Klausmeier 1969) offers a structure for providing friendly definitions of a word along with related characteristics, examples, and nonexamples. The process of stating a definition, describing characteristics, and articulating examples and nonexamples helps students develop a deeper understanding of a word than they might achieve from only a definition. Often used with nouns, the Frayer Model is an especially useful tool in the content areas. The graphics can be developed by the teacher with input from the class and left on display for a period of time, such as throughout a unit of study, or students may work in small groups to complete a graphic for an assigned word (the same word for every group) or words (a different word for each group that will then be introduced to classmates). Additionally, teachers who use word walls (see Chapter 4) may invite students to sketch Frayer Models on the reverse side of the word cards so students can use the cards as a resource for understanding word meanings, if necessary.

An alternative Frayer Model, which is considered more difficult by some because it increases the level of critical analysis required, asks students to provide essential and nonessential characteristics along with examples and nonexamples. Figures 5.4, 5.5, and 5.6 provide samples. Students or the teacher can also draw pictures in the Frayer Model boxes.

After teaching important vocabulary, some teachers supply students with completed Frayer Models with the target word missing. Students provide the term based on the information presented.

**FIGURE 5.4 Frayer Model for** *colony*

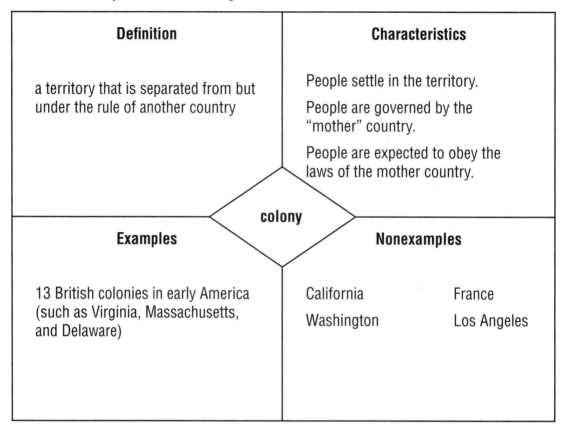

| Definition | Characteristics |
|---|---|
| a territory that is separated from but under the rule of another country | People settle in the territory. People are governed by the "mother" country. People are expected to obey the laws of the mother country. |

**colony**

| Examples | Nonexamples |
|---|---|
| 13 British colonies in early America (such as Virginia, Massachusetts, and Delaware) | California France Washington Los Angeles |

**FIGURE 5.5 Frayer Model for** *precipitation*

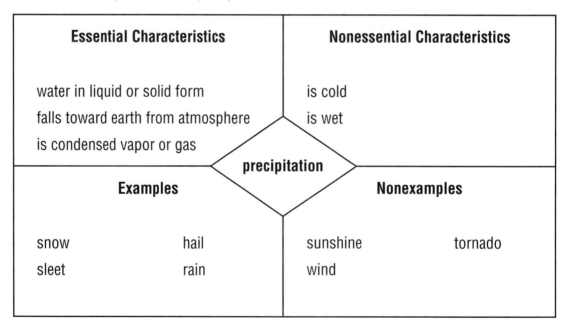

| Essential Characteristics | Nonessential Characteristics |
|---|---|
| water in liquid or solid form falls toward earth from atmosphere is condensed vapor or gas | is cold is wet |

**precipitation**

| Examples | Nonexamples |
|---|---|
| snow        hail  sleet        rain | sunshine        tornado  wind |

**FIGURE 5.6  Frayer Model for *parallelogram***

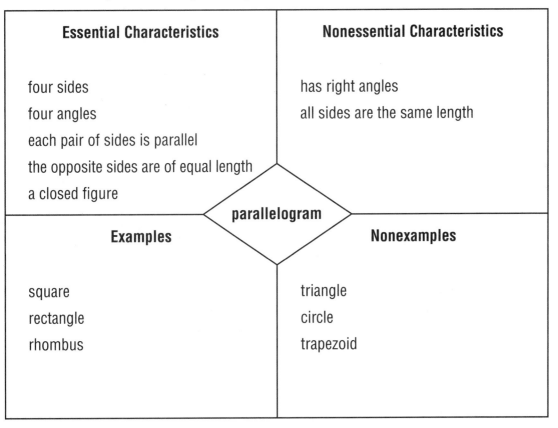

4. **Concept of Definition Map**

Another framework that helps students develop a deep understanding of a word is the Concept of Definition Map. This map was originally described by Schwartz and Raphael (1985) as a strategy for helping students determine the meanings of words from context on their own. First students are taught that several types of information are needed to understand a word. These types of information, or elements of a definition, include the category to which the word belongs, characteristics of the word, and examples. For instance, students are taught that in order to fully understand the word *sandwich*, they should know that it is a food (i.e., category), is made with bread, is filled with something, and often is eaten for lunch (i.e., characteristics), and they should be able to provide examples, such as peanut butter and jelly or grilled cheese. These elements are displayed in a map to provide a visual representation of a word's meaning. For younger children, Schwartz and Raphael translated the elements into the following questions: (1) What is it? (2) What is it like? (3) What are some examples? Figure 5.7 provides a blank map.

After learning the elements vital to understanding a word, students are taught to use the elements or questions to determine whether they know the meaning of a word and to guide their search for information. For example, if students can identify that *amphibians* are animals (i.e., category) but are unable to list characteristics or provide examples, they have identified what it is that they do not know about the word and then can seek out that information. They use available resources, including the context in which the word was used, or tools such as dictionaries, glossaries, and the Internet. Schwartz and Raphael's goal was for students to learn to use the strategy in order to independently acquire word knowledge.

More often, we have seen teachers use Concept of Definition Maps to directly teach words to their students. Teachers sketch a blank Concept of Definition Map on the board, identify a word for exploration, and invite student contributions related to the elements displayed on the map. The teacher records information on the map and encourages students to copy the map and keep it in a vocabulary notebook for easy review and reference. Sometimes, the teacher provides students with blank maps and asks them to work with partners or in small groups to gather information about a word and then share with classmates.

Completing a map requires students to actively engage with a word as they link the new word to known information, consider its relationship to other words or concepts, identify characteristics of the word, and generate examples. As with the other strategies described in this section, the discussion that occurs when students work with classmates on a Concept of Definition Map is an important aspect of the experience. Students clarify their thinking by explaining their ideas to peers, and they refine their understanding of a word's meaning as they develop the map.

**FIGURE 5.7 Concept of Definition Map**

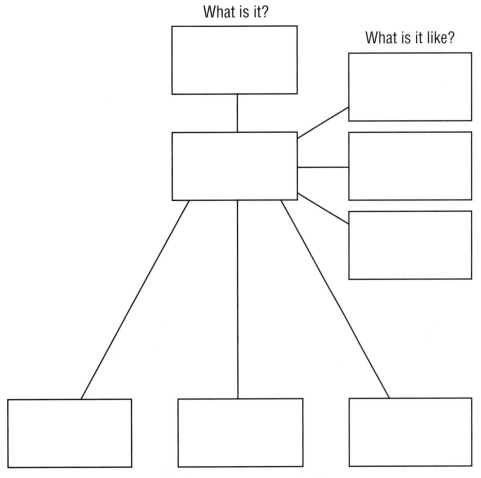

## 5. Verbal and Visual Word Association

The Verbal and Visual Word Association strategy requires students to think about a word in several ways and to record their thinking in boxes, as depicted in figure 5.8. In the upper-left box, students write the target word. In the lower-left box, students write a definition of the word based on a friendly explanation provided by the teacher. To support and enhance their understanding of the word, the teacher asks the students to then draw a picture representation of the word's meaning and to share a personal association related to the word in the remaining two boxes. This strategy provides students with the opportunity to think about a word in multiple ways. Asking the students to work with peers on this task or to share their responses in small groups reinforces and extends their understanding of the word.

Some teachers provide students with index cards, which the students fold into fourths or divide into fourths with lines. The students punch a hole in the upper-left corners of their completed cards, put them on a ring with other words they are collecting, and keep them as a personal "dictionary" for easy reference. Other teachers put students' work on display so the entire class can access a range of verbal and visual representations.

**FIGURE 5.8 Verbal and Visual Word Association**

| | |
|---|---|
| *isolate* | |
| *to put by oneself* | *When I was sick, my mom isolated me from my family members so they wouldn't get sick, too.* |

## 6. Word Maps

Dan had a teacher who frequently introduced words in a reading selection by "mapping" them on the board. Students copied her maps and saved them in individual notebooks for easy access and review. The maps consisted of the following:

Name the word.

Define it.

Provide an example sentence.

Tell what it is like.

This map is similar to the Frayer Model in that it provides a framework for thinking about word meanings and contextual information, including, in this case, the use of the word in a sentence. Sample maps are presented here.

*Finicky*

*Fussy and extremely careful*

*The woman was finicky when it came to what she would eat.*

*Picky, choosy, particular*

---

*Dispute*

*Disagreement*

*My uncle settled the dispute between his sons.*

*Quarrel, fight, difference of opinion, conflict*

---

*Ambled*

*Walked without hurrying*

*Because they weren't in a hurry, they ambled down the street.*

*Strolled, sauntered, moseyed, took their time*

As we noted earlier, when introducing students to new words, it is productive to share a definition, a model of how the word is used, and related words, which is exactly what this teacher did when she provided these maps for her students. Dan's description of her classroom presentation of the maps revealed that she talked to the students about the words, acted out word meanings when possible (e.g., she pretended to reject the contents of a student's lunch bag by wrinkling her nose and handing it back to the student to demonstrate *finicky*), and asked them to help generate the sentences and related words. Students had vivid memories of her presentations, and they had representations of the word meanings in the form of her word maps.

7. **Semantic Feature Analysis**

Several of the strategies we share in this chapter help students understand how words are related to one another. Semantic Feature Analysis shows how words differ. This strategy is often useful in a unit of study where students are presented with several terms that have similar meanings. In figure 5.9, we share a Semantic Feature Analysis for words related to a fourth-grade study of California history. The words all refer to structures built in the days before California became a state. However, because it was important to the teacher that the students understand the differences among the terms, he developed a Semantic Feature Analysis chart with the students' assistance.

**FIGURE 5.9** **Semantic Feature Analysis for early California structures**

| Structure | Early California | Housed American Indians | Served a religious purpose | Served a defense purpose |
|-----------|------------------|-------------------------|----------------------------|--------------------------|
| Mission   |                  |                         |                            |                          |
| Rancheria |                  |                         |                            |                          |
| Pueblo    |                  |                         |                            |                          |
| Presidio  |                  |                         |                            |                          |

After introducing the words with friendly explanations and reading about them in a content-area textbook, the teacher asked the students to think about the words more deeply. He drew a grid on the board and listed the concepts under study down the left side and features he believed would help students appreciate the distinctions among the concepts across the top. He led a discussion about the terms and recorded a plus sign at the appropriate intersection on the grid if the word in the left column had the feature, a minus sign if it did not, and a question mark if it could, under certain circumstances, have the feature. Students were encouraged to use resource materials to determine the features of each term. Figure 5.10 shows how this strategy can be used to analyze geometric shapes.

**FIGURE 5.10 Semantic Feature Analysis for geometric shapes**

| Figure | Three-dimensional | Two-dimensional | Has lines | Has right angles | All sides are of equal length |
|---|---|---|---|---|---|
| Cube | + | − | + | + | + |
| Square | − | + | + | + | + |
| Rectangle | − | + | + | + | ? |

8. **Nonlinguistic Representations**

Dual coding theory (Paivio 1990) suggests that information is stored in memory in the brain in linguistic and nonlinguistic forms. To support students' understanding of words, teachers should provide students with nonlinguistic experiences with the words and concepts they represent, along with verbal explanations. For example, teachers can introduce a word by acting it out or representing its meaning through a drawing or sketch. Students should be engaged in developing nonlinguistic representations of words and might be asked to sketch, paint, sculpt, pantomime, perform, create a tableau representing a word's meaning, or participate in other nonverbal expressions. Several of the strategies in this chapter incorporate a nonlinguistic element.

9. **Vocabulary Self-Collection Strategy**

The Vocabulary Self-Collection Strategy was developed by Haggard (1982) to motivate students to actively engage in word study. In this strategy, students each identify two words they think are important for the class or group to learn. Students select words from any source—a book they are reading, a class discussion, television, the newspaper, or anywhere else. The students bring their words to class and present them to their peers. In a nomination process, students share each word, where they found it, what they think it means, and why they think it is important to know.

The teacher also nominates two words. After hearing about all of the words, the students vote on the words they would like to learn, and the top eight or so are identified. Over the next several days, the teacher uses strategies like those described in this chapter to teach the selected words. The process is repeated the next week, and new words are voted on for study.

Ruddell and Shearer (2002) found that students consistently selected important and challenging words when permitted to choose their own words for study, devoted more effort to learning them, learned them better, and retained them longer than commercially packaged word lists. Ruddell and Shearer argued that when students are given control over the vocabulary curriculum, they are more interested in the words and more willing to invest time into learning them.

Identifying contexts for the words and engaging in social interaction are important aspects of this strategy.

## Reinforcing and Extending Understanding of Words

In order for students to acquire deep and lasting knowledge of words, introducing them to words through friendly explanations and various maps or other strategies is not sufficient. Students must have multiple encounters with the words in a variety of contexts. The strategies described in this section provide students with experiences with words beyond their initial introductions.

1. **Word Sorts**

   Word sorts require students to organize words into meaningful groups. Open sorts invite the students to organize words in whatever way is meaningful to them, and closed sorts provide a structure for the students. Several years ago we witnessed an open sort for several words related to the study of vertebrates that resulted in some students separating the words into the following two groups:

Group 1—*stallion, mare, bull, colt, cow, filly, horse, foal, calf*

Group 2—*rooster, goose, hen, gander, chick, gosling*

When asked to explain their sort, the second-grade students replied that the first group consisted of mammals and the second consisted of birds. Other students grouped the words according to size of animal: large or small. When conducting open sorts, teachers should accept all responses as long as students can explain their sorts and they make sense.

Sometimes teachers like to start with an open sort to allow the students to think in diverse ways about how the words are related to one another and to negotiate sorting criteria with peers. After groups of students have had the opportunity to complete an open sort and hear the thinking of their peers, the teacher then conducts one or more closed sorts based on criteria that he or she believes will enhance students' understanding of the words. Using the animal words above, the teacher we observed asked the students to sort the words according to whether they refer to a male animal, a female animal, or either male or female animals. Most of the students sorted the words as follows:

Group 1—*stallion, bull, rooster, gander, colt* (male)

Group 2—*mare, cow, goose, hen, filly* (female)

Group 3—*horse, foal, calf, chick, gosling* (either)

The teacher and students discussed the sort and students were given the opportunity to move any words they might have placed in the wrong group. Next, the teacher presented the following groupings and asked the students to identify the criterion for the sort:

Group 1—*stallion, hen, rooster, horse, cow, mare, gander, goose, bull*

Group 2—*chick, foal, calf, gosling, colt, filly*

Do you know how the words are sorted? If you think they are adults and offspring, you are absolutely correct! Notice how the teacher got the students to think about word meanings in deep ways. Each word represents not only a particular animal but also the classification of the animal, its sex, and its age, and this became apparent as the students sorted the words according to different criteria.

Recently, one of the author's sons was asked to learn the following words as part of his seventh-grade study of the Middle Ages: *monasteries, feudalism, hierarchies, fiefs, vassals, oath of fealty, knights, homage, manor, serfs, guild.* An open sort of these words completed by small groups of students would likely have yielded interesting conversations about their meanings and their relationships. Students would have had to articulate their understandings of word meanings and determine whether and how the words belong together. Although the teacher did not engage the students in a sort, we asked Dan to sort the words. His response to our request resulted in the following groupings:

| | | |
|---|---|---|
| *vassals* | *monasteries* | *feudalism* |
| *knights* | *fiefs* | *hierarchies* |
| *serfs* | *manor* | *homage* |
| *guild* | | *oath of fealty* |

Dan explained that the first grouping consisted of people or groups of people, the second consisted of places, and the third consisted of systems or practices. This experience not only required Dan to think about what the words mean as individual words but also what they mean in relation to each other, thus supporting the development of a network of understanding about concepts discussed in the unit. It also provided us with insights into his understanding of the terms.

Note that word sorts are flexible tools that can be used at various points in the instructional cycle. Sorting words after they have been introduced and explained serves as an opportunity to review terms and deepen and enrich students' developing understanding of the words. Sorts can also be conducted before a lesson or unit. This requires students to think about what they already know about a topic and helps them identify what they need to learn, thus prompting them to set purposes for the lesson.

If you choose to try word sorts—and we hope you do—consider these suggestions:

- Write sets of words on index cards and put them in baggies for quick and easy distribution. Or type them in a large font on the computer and print them in columns. Have the students cut them apart.

- Try sorting the words yourself before presenting them to students. The experience will help you anticipate the diverse ways students might sort the words if provided the opportunity to complete an open sort, and it will help you identify various criteria for closed sorts.

- When conducting an open sort, be accepting of students' ideas. There is not a single right answer to an open sort. Open sorts are intended to elicit diverse responses. However, if students adopt a criterion and then place one or more words in the wrong group (e.g., *foal* in the adult group), you will want to assist them in moving the word into the correct group. Sometimes, allowing groups to explain their sorts to other groups before sharing with the class as a whole can be a productive way to check the students' sorts.

2. **Content Links**

Content Links, also known as Word Links (Yopp 2007), is another strategy that requires students to think about the meanings of words and whether and how words connect to one another. To prepare, the teacher generates a list of words related to a unit of study or piece of literature the students have read. Ideally, he or she selects as many words as there are students in the class. For example, a life sciences teacher might identify the following words from a unit on ecology: *food chain, food web, trophic level, phosphorus cycle, nitrogen cycle, carbon cycle, habitat, biosphere, biome, ecosystem, biological community, population, niche, abiotic factors, biotic factors, symbiosis, parasitism, commensalism, mutualism, autotroph, scavengers, heterotroph, herbivore, omnivore, decomposer, carnivore,* and *organism.* These words are all highly relevant to the recent unit and have been previously defined and discussed.

The teacher records each word on a large word card, such as a half sheet or full sheet of copy paper or cardstock. The word cards are distributed so that each student receives one. Each student reads his or her words and circulates through the room to identify a classmate with whom to link. The goal for each student is to find a partner whose word is related to his or her own in some way. Students talk to each other about the relationship between their words as they consider whether to form a partnership.

After all students have found a partner, they share their words with the rest of the class, explain what the words mean, and describe how the words fit together. The student holding the term *biotic factors* might choose to link with the student holding the term *abiotic factors*, explaining that together they constitute an ecosystem. The student holding *biological community* might link with the student holding *population* because communities are made up of two or more populations living in the same area. After all students share their word links, the teacher asks them to break their links and find a new partner. Once again, the students walk through the room discussing their words with each other, deciding with whom to link, and then sharing their thinking. As a final step, the teacher can ask the students to form word clusters where four students share how all of their words are connected. Or, if the particular set of words is suited to the request, the teacher can ask the students to create hierarchical groupings. Sometimes we support this step by printing the words on different-colored cards. In our study of vertebrates, for example, the word *vertebrate* might be printed on green paper or cardstock, the words *amphibian, mammal, bird, reptile,* and *fish* on yellow paper, and specific animals on orange paper. How might you color code the following mathematical terms?

| | |
|---|---|
| *one-dimensional figure* | *two-dimensional figure* |
| *cube* | *trapezoid* |
| *parallelogram* | *triangle* |
| *circle* | *cone* |
| *sphere* | *right triangle* |
| *square* | *rectangle* |
| *pyramid* | *cylinder* |

Word cards should be saved, as they are often useful with other units of study. Consider slipping each card into a clear plastic sleeve for protection from the wear and tear that results from repeated use and putting the cards in a notebook for easy storage and access.

### 3. Carousels

Carousels actively engage students in thinking and talking about words and are an effective way to provide and reinforce definitional and contextual information. Just as the name implies, carousels require students to rotate around the classroom—like a carousel—moving from one posted vocabulary chart to another and completing a task at each chart. There are various ways to conduct a carousel, and we share four here. Regardless of the variation you utilize, you will first need to think about how you will organize students into groups. One way is to merely ask students to stand by a chart of their choice, requesting that they evenly distribute themselves among the charts. The teacher may have to make friendly requests that a couple of students move to another chart if they cluster themselves unevenly. This ensures that every chart has a group and no group is too large. Alternatively, the teacher can assign students to a chart. For example, the students at table group 1 can be asked to stand by one chart, the students from table group 2 can be asked to stand by another, and so forth, or the teacher might strategically distribute students who are likely to need assistance or are likely to be able to provide assistance to their group.

In all of the variations, the idea is that student groups will complete a task at the chart in a short amount of time and then, at a signal, move to the next chart in the room to complete the next task. The rotation continues until all groups have visited all the charts.

**Same Word, Different Task**—In this version, all students consider the same word, and the task at each chart is different. The teacher announces to her fourth graders, for example, that the word is *migration*, chosen because of its use in a recent social studies unit. At a signal, students at a chart titled "Definition" collaborate to come up with a definition of *migration*. A group member records the definition on the chart. Students at a chart titled "Sentence" work together to generate a sentence that incorporates the word and then write it on the chart. The tasks assigned at the remaining charts might include the following:

- Synonyms: Write a synonym or closely related word on the chart.

- Antonyms: Write an antonym or close opposite.

- Picture: Draw a picture that represents the word's meaning.

- Context: Provide an example of where you might see this word in print or hear it used (e.g., in a history book, at a party, in a travel brochure).

- Graphic Organizer: Develop a graphic organizer that conveys information about the word.

Groups complete their first tasks and wait by the chart until the teacher signals that it is time to rotate in a clockwise or counterclockwise direction to the next chart. There, they read the work posted by the previous group and then add to the chart. Students who wrote a definition on the first chart are now writing a sentence on the sentence chart. Students who wrote a sentence at their first chart are now generating a synonym for the synonym chart. Students may not duplicate the work of the previous group; they must think of a new way to state the definition or add to or refine the definition, they must generate a different sentence, they must write another synonym or antonym, and so forth. At the chart labeled "Graphic Organizer," each group continues the work begun by the first group on a single graphic organizer, with each successive group adding to the graphic organizer, perhaps providing an additional example or adding a link and new category. Or you might allow students to generate an alternate graphic organizer if they have a different vision.

At the end of the carousel rotation, each group will have contributed to every chart. This activity encourages students to think about a single word in various ways and gives them the opportunity to view the ideas of the groups that cycled to the charts before them.

**Different Words, Same Task**—In this version of the carousel strategy, a different word is posted on each chart. Each group draws a task card from a deck (see the sample tasks listed above) and engages in the same task at every word chart they visit. Thus, one group of fourth-grade students will define *migration* at the first chart, for example, define *economy* at the second chart, define *transcontinental* at the third chart, and so forth. Another group will use *migration* in a sentence at the first chart, write a sentence including *economy* on the second chart, and use the remaining words in sentences at their respective charts. By the time the students have completed the carousel, they will have responded to several words in the same way. Each chart will display a wealth of information about a word, and the charts should all be shared at the conclusion of the carousel.

**Different Words, Different Tasks**—This version is our favorite. It provides an opportunity for students to think about several words in different ways. However, it can be difficult, especially for younger children, so be sure to prepare the students by thoroughly explaining the process and perhaps slowly walking students through the first two rotations.

In this version, each chart posted in the carousel displays a different vocabulary word that the class has studied. At their first chart, every group writes a definition of the word presented on the chart before them. At their second chart, every group views the new word, reads the definition provided by the previous group, and then uses the word in a sentence. At their third chart, all groups read the word, the definition, and the sentence appearing on the chart and write a synonym or two for the word. Thus, students are not thinking about the same word in various ways (the first version above) or thinking about different words in the same way (second version above). Instead, they are thinking about a different word and completing a different task with each rotation. It is complicated, but powerful! Students in the upper elementary grades and higher can easily complete this carousel with appropriate explanation and support.

**Frayer Model**—The teacher posts large copies of blank Frayer Models (see pages 130–131) around the room, each with a different word. Groups of students rotate from chart to chart, adding information to each chart. The students complete the same task at each chart (e.g., write the definition or generate an example or nonexample) or complete a different portion of the chart for each new word. Because the Frayer Model only includes four boxes, the charts will be complete after four rotations. Thus, students will not have the opportunity to record information on every chart. However, if you provide time for students to return to their original charts, review the contributions of classmates, and present the charts to the class as a whole, all students will have had the opportunity to hear each word discussed.

Usually it is effective to have group sizes of no more than four or five, so depending on the number of students in the class, you will want to be deliberate about the number of words or tasks you select for your carousel. For a class of 30, for example, seven charts, which would result in five groups of four and two groups of five, might be appropriate. Talking to peers about what words mean and how to use them not only actively engages students in talking about the words you want them to learn but also provides them with opportunities to hear different perspectives and ideas about what words mean and how they are used. Additionally, English language learners will benefit from meaningful interactions about words in a safe setting that provides them with authentic reasons to communicate orally. However, in order for a carousel to be a successful experience for all students, the teacher must ensure that students have had sufficient experience with the words. This strategy should not be used to introduce words but rather to reinforce and extend understandings of word meanings.

Each teacher will need to be the judge of how much time to allow the groups at the charts. We often limit discussions and writing to one or two minutes per chart because we find that students maintain a high level of engagement if the pace is reasonably fast but not so fast as to be frustrating. Likewise, you will want to be deliberate about the tasks included in the carousel. Some tasks will take less time than others, and you do not want groups standing around too long.

The teacher will also want to decide in advance whether students will be permitted to correct any errors they note were made on the charts by previous groups. For example, what will students do if the previous group does not define the word accurately? You may want to carefully attend to the work of the groups and deal with errors promptly.

Additionally, the teacher will need to decide whether to assign each group a different color of marker for recording responses. Use of different-colored markers makes tracking the authors of any contribution easy, which may be useful for applauding a group's interesting contribution, providing feedback to students, or asking a group to elaborate on its thinking. The classroom must be a safe place, however, for this kind of public response to students' work.

4. **Linear Arrays**

Linear Arrays, also known as semantic gradients, are useful when students are learning adjectives and adverbs for which there are scalar antonyms. Unlike polar antonyms, which are dichotomous, scalar antonyms allow for gradations

(Powell 1986). The terms *hot, warm, tepid, cool*, and *cold* are scalar antonyms because they represent a range of meanings, including a neutral term. In this sample list of words, *tepid* might be targeted for instruction. The teacher provides a friendly explanation of tepid, telling the students that it is a temperature that is neither hot nor cold and is often used to refer to the degree of warmth of a liquid. Tepid water is approximately room temperature; it is lukewarm. The teacher tells the students that for maximum cleanliness, they should wash their hands with warm, not tepid, water. The teacher asks whether anyone has ever eaten tepid soup and whether they liked it. To reinforce the students' understanding of the word, the teacher randomly distributes five cards with the words *hot, cold, cool, tepid*, and *warm* printed in large letters on them. He or she asks the five students holding the cards to stand at the front of the room and invites the rest of the class to put the five students in an order that makes sense or that ranges from one extreme to the other. The class tells the five students how to position themselves, explaining their reasons for the order.

Given the target word *bland*, the teacher might ask the students to order these words: *delicious, bland, tasty*, and *unappetizing*. The opportunity to put the words in order requires them to think about words in the context of related words and provides them with a better sense of the words' meanings.

The high school daughter of one of the authors recently read a war story. To ensure that her daughter understood an important event in the story, Erica's mother explained the ranks of several of the officers. She then wrote the terms *major, colonel, general, corporal*, and *captain* on index cards and asked Erica to place them in order. The task helped clarify the hierarchy of the officers' ranks, and Erica's new understanding of the terms led her to a different appreciation for the story, in which a corporal yelled at a major. The courage (or foolishness) displayed by the corporal who shouted at a superior officer became transparent. (The linear array she correctly generated was, from lowest to highest rank, as follows: *corporal, captain, major, colonel, general*.)

5. **Ten Important Words Plus**

An enhancement of the Ten Important Words strategy described in Chapter 4, Ten Important Words Plus furthers student thinking about words that carry important meaning in a text (H. K. Yopp and Yopp 2007; R. H. Yopp and Yopp 2007). After students write a summary sentence, the teacher or students select several words for discussion. The teacher distributes colored cards that contain different tasks, and students meet with two or three peers who are holding cards of the same color. For example, the teacher might select the word *population* from a reading about the impact of humans on the environment. The task on the blue card reads, "Think of as many other forms of this word as you can. For example, forms of *happy* include *happiness, happiest, unhappy*." Students with blue cards meet in small groups to generate a response to this task and prepare to share their answer with the entire class.

Simultaneously, students with yellow cards prepare a response to the task, "List synonyms for the word or words highly related in meaning." Students with green cards prepare a response to the task, "Generate sentences in which you use the word. One sentence should relate to the content of the text. Other sentences should use the word in a different context."

Additional tasks might include the following:

- List antonyms or close opposites.

- Identify where you might expect to see or hear this word. Be specific. For example, you might expect to find the word *sparkling* in an advertisement for jewelry. Where else?

- Use a dictionary and share a definition or definitions of the word. Note multiple meanings, if any.

- Draw a picture that conveys the meaning of the word.

- Act out the word.

- Create a semantic map of the word, displaying it in relation to other words of your choice.

- Share a connection between this word and something in your life.

- Return to the text and find one or more sentences in which the word is used. Explain the meaning of the sentence(s) you find. Comment on any text clues the author provided to make the meaning clear.

Each small group of students shares its responses with the class, and then another word from the reading is selected. Students again discuss the task in their small groups and share their responses with the whole class. After the students have completed the same task with two or three different words, the teacher asks them to exchange cards with someone who has a different color. This gives students an opportunity to meet with different students and complete a different task.

Teachers must remember that not all words are a good match for all tasks. For example, it might be difficult for students to generate different forms of some words or identify synonyms for other words. Sometimes we put two tasks on a colored card, one on the front and one on the back, and instruct students to complete the task on the front for the first word we assign and the task on the back for the second if it is a more appropriate task for the word.

Ten Important Words Plus actively engages students in thinking and talking about words, their meanings, and the contexts in which they are used. Students read the words, identify those words that are significant to the content of the text, talk about them, write sentences, and then examine them in finer ways through the "Plus" portion of the Ten Important Words Plus strategy. We have found this strategy to provide rich experiences with words that enhance students' understanding of the words as well as their understanding of the text in which they were found.

## Using Words

In addition to thoughtful introduction to words followed by multiple exposures to them, students need many opportunities and reasons to apply words they are learning. Because it is unlikely that students will spontaneously begin to use new words, the teacher must structure experiences that necessitate their use.

### 1. Oral Presentations

One way to prompt the use of new words is to ask students to prepare presentations related to the content in which the words are embedded. For example, if students learned the words *fault*, *fold*, and *wave* in their study of earthquakes, assigning them to prepare and deliver oral presentations about topics related to earthquakes will prompt them to use both general academic and specialized content vocabulary. Students will review the material, prepare their presentations, rehearse them, and then present them. At each stage of the process, they think about and utilize the target words. Asking them to include visuals in their presentations, such as diagrams and illustrations, further supports their understanding of the words and will reinforce their classmates' understanding as well. Presentations can take several forms, including electronic presentations (such as *PowerPoint*®), reader's theater presentations, and speeches.

## 2. Bookmaking and Other Written Presentations

Students who are asked to write in response to a unit of study or reading selection will incorporate words that are important to the topic. Many teachers like to have students summarize or expand their learning by constructing books. There are many resources available to teachers that detail the steps involved in constructing various types of books. We briefly describe two bookmaking ideas here.

- Alphabet books are useful for prompting students to use academic vocabulary. In these books, students share information about the topic, one page for each letter of the alphabet. Students review resources for relevant words and then explain each term using the format of "*C* is for community. A community is ... "

- If students have learned words selected from a narrative text, they can retell the story, describing the setting, characters, problem, climax, and resolution in an accordion book, in which pages of the book are taped together in such a way that they can be folded like an accordion. Accordion books are excellent group projects, and students are likely to use important words they have learned in their retelling. Students work together to conceptualize the book, and then each student is responsible for developing one page of the book.

Writing Roulette is a strategy in which the teacher identifies four or five words that students must use in a piece of writing. Students, sitting in small groups, each begin writing, with the task being to use at least one of the target words in the first few sentences. The teacher calls time after several minutes, and the students pass their incomplete papers to the person on their right. Students read the work begun by their classmate and add to the composition. Their charge is to incorporate a different target word into the work. The paper is passed two or three more times until all students in the group have added to each piece of writing. The last writer ensures that all target words have been used. Each written product is shared with the group. Typically, interest is high, as all group members have contributed to the products. The group may wish to select one of the works to share with the entire class.

Various forms of poetry also provide interesting opportunities for students to use target words. These two haiku poems were developed by second graders who completed a study of the rainforest. The students drew from the vocabulary that was part of their unit of study.

*Rainforest layers*

*Forest floor, understory,*

*Canopy above.*

*Near the equator*

*Tropical rainforests grow*

*Wet, warm, colorful.*

Motivation for learning and using words is increased when students express themselves in writing (Scott and Nagy 2004). Word choice becomes important as students attempt to share their ideas with an audience, and so the students— like all writers—are more thoughtful and deliberate in their use of language.

# Conclusion

Although students' vocabularies appear to increase dramatically as a result of incidental learning opportunities over the years of their schooling, explicit instruction of word meanings in every area of the curriculum is an essential component of an effective vocabulary program. This is true for all students but especially students who are most in need of enhancing their vocabularies.

Indeed, Beck, McKeown, and Kucan (2002) argued that relying on incidental learning that occurs through wide reading may add to the inequities in vocabulary knowledge because struggling readers do not read well enough to read widely.

In this chapter, we provided a wealth of strategies for teaching and extending students' understanding of words that the teacher—or the students—selects as worthy of instruction. Words should be introduced through friendly explanations, in meaningful contexts, and with activities that highlight relationships among words. Initial experiences with words should be followed by activities that extend and deepen students' understanding and provide opportunities for students to think about words in different contexts. Finally, teachers should implement strategies that require students to use words—in discussions, in presentations, and in their writing—so they come to truly own them. Repeated exposure to the words in many contexts is key to word learning.

# Think About It!

1. Revisit your ratings of the terms at the beginning of this chapter. How would you rate your understanding now?

2. Select a strategy described in this chapter and explain how it is grounded in principles of good vocabulary instruction.

3. Select a chapter from a content-area text or a work of literature that you are about to share with your students. What vocabulary will you select for instruction? How will you introduce these words? How will you reinforce and extend student understanding of these words? How will you engage students in applying the words to new contexts?

# Chapter 6

# Teaching Word-Learning Strategies

## Make a Match

It is quite possible that you have never seen the words in Column A before. Nevertheless, do your best to match them with their definitions in Column B.

| Column A | Column B |
|----------|----------|
| quadricentennial | between two vowels |
| postorbital | below the timberline |
| subalpine | fear of numbers |
| supernumerary | 400th anniversary |
| intervocalic | more than the required number |
| arithmophobia | behind the eye socket |

How did you do? How confident are you of your matches? Why might you understand these words despite never seeing them before?

Now read the following sentences. Notice the italicized words. Can you infer their meanings?

- Using a rake, he *ted* the newly mown pile of grass thinly throughout his yard in the hope that it would dry quickly.

- She later wondered if she had given coherent responses to her father, as her new cold medication left her *muzzy*.

- Never seen laughing, he was a true *agelast*.

- The *chirotonsor's* customers were his best advertisement; their haircuts consistently received compliments.

If you believe you understood each of these sentences, give yourself a pat on the back! You are an independent word learner!

*"When it comes to words, every person is destined to be a lifelong learner."*

—Dale Johnson (2001, 9)

Explicit teaching of words is important, and in Chapter 5, we provided many strategies for vocabulary instruction. Given the sheer number of words in the English language, however, it is virtually impossible to teach them all directly. There are not enough hours in the school day, days in a school year, or years in a school career to provide sufficient instruction in word meanings to adequately build students' vocabularies. Fortunately, as we noted earlier, a sizeable portion of students' vocabularies is acquired through exposure to language, and in Chapters 2 and 3, we discussed how to increase students' exposure to rich oral and written language. Yet, some students may learn more efficiently from exposure than others. Perhaps these are the students who have an interest in words and are inspired by adults who provide word-conscious environments such as those described in Chapter 4.

In this chapter, we address an important complement to explicit instruction in word meanings, exposure to language, and stimulating an interest in words—that is, equipping students with independent word-learning strategies. Specifically, we discuss the role of morphological knowledge (i.e., knowledge of the parts of words that contribute to meaning) in helping students derive word meanings, and we explore the use of context to infer the meaning of unknown words. We also share thoughts on supporting students' use of the dictionary to help them learn word meanings. Building skill in these word-learning strategies increases students' potential for learning words independently, and independent word-learning abilities should be a goal for every student (Baumann et al. 2003; Nagy, Berninger, and Abbott 2006).

# Morphology

More than half of English words are morphologically complex; that is they contain more than one meaningful element. The meanings of many of these words can be inferred from the meaning of their parts (Nagy et al. 2006). For instance, if you know what it means to be *kind* and you know what *un-* means, then it is likely that you will understand the meaning of the word *unkind*. Once you have learned the meaning of the prefix *un-*, you do not need to be directly taught words such as *unavailable*, *unhappy*, *unforgiving*, and *unstoppable* if you know what *available, happy, forgiving*, and *stoppable* mean. Understanding the role of one unit, in this case *un-*, pays considerable dividends! Likewise, if you know that *bio-* means "life" and *-graphy* has to do with writing, then you likely can infer that the word *biography* refers to a written account of someone's life. If you know that *geo-* refers to the earth and *-centric* means "center" or "middle," then you know that the term *geocentric* refers to something with earth at the center. The geocentric view of the universe—one that predominated thinking for centuries—held that the earth was the center of the universe.

Your ability to successfully match the words at the beginning of this chapter with their definitions suggests that you used your knowledge of word parts to infer the meanings of the words. Wonderful! This strategy—thinking about word parts to determine the meaning of a word—empowers you to understand many more words than you have been explicitly taught. Had you ever heard the word *supernumerary*? Probably not. Yet you likely know that *super* means "extra," "more than," or "over and above" (think of *supermarket, superhuman, superpower*, and *supersonic*) and that *numerary* is related to the word *number*. Voila! *Supernumerary* means "having extra or more than the number you need."

Because the parts of a word often provide clues to the word's meaning, an important component of vocabulary instruction is the examination of meaningful word parts. We begin this section by defining the parts of words that provide clues to meaning. Next we share principles for instruction, and then we describe several strategies for teaching word parts as a way of supporting vocabulary development.

## Morphemes

Morphemes are the smallest units of meaning that make up the words in a language. For example, the word *happy,* which has five graphemes (i.e., written symbols, or letters) and four phonemes (i.e., sounds), has a single morpheme; there is one unit of meaning in this word. On the other hand, the word *unhappy* has two morphemes: the unit *un-*, which carries the meaning "not," and the unit *happy.* The word *friend* has a single morpheme, whereas the word *friends* has two morphemes: the unit *friend* and the unit *-s*, which signifies a plural. Likewise, the word *friend's* has two morphemes: the unit *friend*, and the unit *'s*, which signifies ownership. As you might guess, words can have one, two, or more morphemes. For instance, *disliked* has three morphemes: *dis-*, signifying "not," *lik(e)*, and *-ed*, signifying past tense. Similarly, the word *teachers* has three morphemes: *teach*, *-er*, signifying "a person who," and *-s*, signifying plural.

Do you notice differences among the morphemes we shared in the previous paragraph? We'll repeat the morphemes here: *happy, un-, friend, -s, 's, dis-, like, -ed, teach, -er.* If you were to sort these morphemes into two groups, you likely would put *happy, friend, like,* and *teach* in one group and *un-, -s, 's, -ed,* and *-er* in another group. How are the morphemes *happy, friend, like,* and *teach* similar? How are the morphemes *un-, dis-, -s, 's,* and *-ed* similar? How are these two groups of morphemes dissimilar? You are correct if you noticed that the morphemes in the first set (*happy, friend, like, teach*) are words, and the morphemes in the second set (*un-, -s, 's, -ed, -er*) are not. Morphemes can be classified as either "free" or "bound." Free morphemes are those that can stand alone as words, as in the case of the morphemes *friend, happy, like,* and *teach.* Bound morphemes cannot stand alone; they must be attached (or bound) to another morpheme.

The morphemes *un-* in *unhappy, -s* in *friends, 's* in *friend's, dis-* and *-ed* in *disliked* and *-er* and *-s* in *teachers* are examples of bound morphemes.

Look at the words below. How many morphemes does each word contain? Name the free morphemes. Name the bound morphemes. We will help with the first one.

*Incomplete*—There are two morphemes: *in-* and *complete*. *Complete* is a free morpheme. *In-* is a bound morpheme (i.e., as used here, it cannot stand alone as a word).

*understandable*

*sadness*

*unquestioning*

*suspiciously*

*looked*

*printer*

*unsuccessfully*

*infinitely*

## Compound Words

Compound words are words composed of two or more free morphemes that take on a single meaning that retains some of the meaning of the original words. Examples are *raincoat* and *houseboat*. If students know the meaning of the word *rain* and the meaning of the word *coat*, they will likely be able to determine the meaning of the word *raincoat*: an outer garment worn in the rain. Some common compound words are listed in figure 6.1. An understanding of the two parts of each of these words allows students to understand the compound word.

**FIGURE 6.1 Sample compound words**

| Word 1 | Word 2 | Compound Word |
|--------|--------|---------------|
| after | noon | afternoon |
| air | plane | airplane |
| basket | ball | basketball |
| bee | hive | beehive |
| break | fast | breakfast |
| business | person | businessperson |
| butter | milk | buttermilk |
| cheese | burger | cheeseburger |
| cow | boy | cowboy |
| finger | print | fingerprint |
| flash | light | flashlight |
| flower | pot | flowerpot |
| gold | fish | goldfish |
| house | boat | houseboat |
| mountain | side | mountainside |
| over | board | overboard |
| pan | cake | pancake |
| rain | coat | raincoat |
| rattle | snake | rattlesnake |
| sail | boat | sailboat |
| scare | crow | scarecrow |
| sky | scraper | skyscraper |
| sun | light | sunlight |
| towns | people | townspeople |
| water | melon | watermelon |

# Word Roots and Base Words

A root is the part of the word that carries most of the word's meaning. The root is the heart of the word, the element from which other words may be constructed, such as when affixes (i.e., prefixes and suffixes) or other roots are added. What are the roots of these words: *running, unlivable, happiness*? Did you say *run, live,* and *happy*? These roots are called free morphemes. When you strip off the affixes, what is left (with slight spelling modifications) are words that can exist on their own.

Sometimes, word roots are bound morphemes, that is, they cannot stand alone. For instance, *mem* and *nym* are the roots in *memory* and *synonym*, respectively. They carry the primary meaning in the words, so they are considered roots even though they cannot stand alone. *Aud* is the root in *audible* and *audition*. Remove the affix from these words and what remains is not a word.

Many educators use the terms *root* and *base* as synonyms. Other scholars call only free morphemes *base words.* Bound morphemes would not be considered bases by these educators. In contrast to both of these views, linguists use the term *root* as an umbrella term that incorporates the sub-category of *base*. This academic discipline considers any part of a word that holds meaning to be a *root*, even affixes. For example, the prefix *un-* changes the meaning of a word to negative and would be considered a root by linguists. Linguists call the main part of the word (the part to which the affixes are added) the *base* whether or not it can stand alone. Regardless of the terminology you wish to use, it is important for students to understand that many words can be broken into parts and the meanings of those parts help unlock the definition of the word.

Over 60 percent of the English language is drawn from Latin and Greek origin. Time spent exploring Latin and Greek roots will help with vocabulary development. Some common Latin and Greek roots are shared in figures 6.2 and 6.3. Knowing the meaning of these roots will aid understanding of new words that contain these roots. For instance, if we know that *astro* has something to do with stars, when we confront the word *astronomer*, we might infer that the word refers to a person who studies the stars—and we would be correct!

**FIGURE 6.2 Common Latin roots**

| Latin Root | Meaning | Sample Words |
|---|---|---|
| aud | to hear | audible, auditorium, audition |
| dict | to speak, to tell | contradict, dictate, diction, predict |
| gress | to walk | digress, progress, transgress |
| ject | to throw | eject, inject, interject, project, reject, subject |
| min | little | minimal, minimum |
| mis, mit | to send | mission, transmit, missile |
| mov, mot | to move | movement, motion |
| ped, pod | foot | pedestrian, pedal, podiatrist, gastropod |
| pend | to hang | append, depend, impend, pendant, pendulum |
| port | to carry | comport, deport, export, import, report, support |
| rupt | to break | interrupt, disrupt, erupt, rupture |
| scrib, script | to write | describe, description, manuscript, prescribe, prescription, scribble, subscribe, transcribe, transcription |
| spect, spic | to see | inspect, conspicuous, spectacles, spectator |
| struct | to build, to form | construct, destruct, instruct, structure |
| tract | to pull, to drag, to draw | attract, contract, detract, extract, protract, retract, traction |
| vert | to turn | convert, divert, invert, revert |
| vid, vis | to see | vision, television, visible |

**FIGURE 6.3  Common Greek roots**

| Greek Root | Meaning | Sample Words |
|---|---|---|
| anthrop | human | misanthrope, philanthropy, anthropomorphic |
| astro | star | astronaut, astronomy, astrology, astrophysics |
| bio | life | biography, biology, biosphere |
| chron | time | anachronism, chronic, chronicle, synchronize, chronometer |
| dem | people | democracy, demography, demagogue, endemic, pandemic |
| geo | Earth | geology, geography |
| meter | measure | thermometer |
| morph | form | amorphous, metamorphic, morphology |
| path | feeling, suffering | empathy, sympathy, apathy, apathetic, psychopathic |
| philo, phil | having a strong affinity or love for | philanthropy, philharmonic, philosophy |
| phon | sound | microphone, telephone, polyphonic, cacophony, phoneme, phonics |
| tele | far, distant | telescope, telecommunicate, telephone, telegraph |

## Affixes

Affixes (from the Latin *affixus*, meaning "to fasten") are bound morphemes that are attached (or fastened) to a root to modify its meaning or change its grammatical function. When an affix is added to the beginning of a word, it is called a prefix. When an affix is added to the end of a word, it is called a suffix.

## Prefixes

Prefixes are bound morphemes attached to the beginning of a root word. *Re-* in *redo*, *un-* in *uncooperative*, and *pre-* in *pregame* are prefixes. How do they modify the meanings of the words *do, cooperative,* and *game*? If you know what each of the prefixes means and you know what the roots mean, then you likely can determine what the new words mean without having to be taught them directly.

White, Sowell, and Yanagihara (1989) identified the 20 most frequently occurring prefixes in American school English for grades 3–9 and noted that these prefixes account for 97 percent of prefix usage. These 20 prefixes are displayed in figure 6.4. Particularly notable is that the first four prefixes account for a large proportion (58 percent) of prefix usage. It is very beneficial for students to learn all of these prefixes.

**FIGURE 6.4 Most common prefixes**

| Prefix* | Percentage* | Selected Meanings | Examples |
|---|---|---|---|
| un- | 26% | not<br><br>reverse, or do the opposite | unhappy<br><br>untie |
| re- | 14% | again<br><br>back | reexamine<br><br>repay |
| in-, im-, ir-, il- | 11% | not | inappropriate, impossible, irreversible, illiterate |
| dis- | 7% | not<br><br>reverse, or do the opposite | dislike<br><br>disconnect |
| en-, em- | 4% | in, into<br><br>to cause to be | ensnare, encircle<br><br>enslave, enable |
| non- | 4% | not | nonviolent |
| in-, im- | 4% | in or into | insight |
| over- | 3% | too much | overdo |
| mis- | 3% | wrong, incorrect | misbehave |
| sub- | 3% | below, beneath | submarine |
| pre- | 3% | before | preschool |
| inter- | 3% | between, among | international |
| fore- | 3% | before in time<br><br>front | forecast<br><br>forehead, foremast |
| de- | 2% | removal<br><br>negate | decontaminate |

| Prefix* | Percentage* | Selected Meanings | Examples |
| --- | --- | --- | --- |
| trans- | 2% | across or over, change | transport transcontinental transform, transcribe |
| super- | 1% | over or above | superman, superscript |
| semi- | 1% | half, partly | semicircle semiskilled |
| anti- | 1% | opposed | antislavery |
| mid- | 1% | middle | midnight |
| under- | 1% | too little | undercooked |

\* from White et al. 1989

## Suffixes

Suffixes are bound morphemes that are added to the end of word roots. There are two types of suffixes: inflectional and derivational. Inflectional suffixes change the tense or number of a word or denote a comparison. For instance, *-ed* is typically used to make a verb past tense, as in the change from *jump* to *jumped*. The suffix *-s* is often used to change number, as in *cat* to *cats*. The inflectional suffixes *-er* and *-est* are added to a root such as *fast* to form *faster* and *fastest*. Derivational suffixes are those that change a word's grammatical function. For instance, when the suffix *-less* is added to the end of *hope* to form *hopeless*, the word's part of speech changes from a noun (or verb) to an adjective. When the suffix *-ly* is added to the end of *glad* to form *gladly*, the word changes from an adjective to an adverb. The meaning can also change significantly, as in the case of *hope* and *hopeless*. Figure 6.5 presents the 20 most common suffixes (White et al. 1989). Note that *-s*, *-es*, *-ed*, and *-ing* (all inflectional suffixes) account for about two-thirds of suffix usage.

**FIGURE 6.5  Most common suffixes**

| Suffix* | Percentage* | Selected Meanings | Examples |
|---|---|---|---|
| -s, -es | 31% | plural<br>verb form | cats, houses,<br>plays, runs |
| -ed | 20% | past-tense verbs | played, hibernated |
| -ing | 14% | verb form (present participle) | jumping |
| -ly | 7% | characteristic of | gladly |
| -er, -or | 4% | a person who | runner, inventor |
| -ion,<br>-tion<br>-ation,<br>-ition | 4% | the act of, process | construction,<br>persecution |
| -ible,<br>-able | 2% | is<br>can be | audible<br>reliable |
| -y | 1% | characterized by | slimy, chewy, cheery |
| -ness | 1% | having | happiness, boldness |
| -ity, -ty | 1% | state of | sanity |
| -ment | 1% | state of | contentment |
| -ic | 1% | having characteristics of | metallic, acidic |
| -ous,<br>-eous,<br>-ious | 1% | having, full of | joyous, dangerous,<br>courageous, curious |
| -en | 1% | made of | silken, wooden |

| Suffix* | Percentage* | Selected Meanings | Examples |
|---|---|---|---|
| -er | 1% | comparative | happier, bigger |
| -ive, -ative, -itive | 1% | being | creative, imaginative |
| -ful | 1% | full of, having | thankful |
| -less | 1% | without | hopeless |
| -est | 1% | comparative | happiest, biggest |

\* from White et al. 1989

So here's what you now know:

Given this word: *prediction*

*pre-*: prefix (bound morpheme) meaning "before"

*dict*: root word (but not a base word) from Latin meaning "tell"

*-tion*: derivational suffix (bound morpheme) indicating "the act of"

*Prediction* is the act of telling beforehand.

Here is the word in a sentence: The weather forecaster's *prediction* about the weekend weather was accurate.

# Principles of Teaching Morphemic Analysis

You may now be asking yourself, "So what? Why should I know about roots, inflected words, and derived words?" As we noted earlier, students' knowledge of morphology is related to vocabulary acquisition (McBride-Chang et al. 2005), and students benefit from instruction in morphology. Thus, teaching word parts and how to use them to make meaning is an important component of a vocabulary program. The more you know about morphology, the more you can help your students develop their vocabularies.

Findings from research on the development of morphological awareness are illuminating and have implications for instruction. Think about the following (see Kieffer and Lesaux 2007; Kuo and Anderson 2006):

- Students understand the relationship between words and their inflected forms at a younger age than they understand the relationship between words and their derived forms. In other words, they recognize the relationship between *use* and *used*, for example, before they recognize the relationship between *use* and *useful*.

- Children as young as preschoolers begin to demonstrate morphological awareness of inflected endings (e.g., adding *-s* to denote a plural, adding *-ed* to denote past tense) and simple compounds. Acquisition of most inflectional forms is generally completed by the early elementary grades.

- Awareness of derivational forms and more complex compounds develops during the upper elementary years and continues through the high school years.

- Derived and inflected words that maintain rather than change the spelling of the word root are more obviously related and therefore easier for students to recognize as related words. For instance, it is relatively easy to glean the relationship between the written word *difficulty* and its root, *difficult*, because the root *difficult* is clearly a part of the word *difficulty*. The written word *depth*, however, is less obviously related to its root, *deep*, because the spelling changes. Likewise, *four* is more obviously related to *fourth* than *five* is to *fifth*.

- Derived and inflected words that maintain rather than change the pronunciation of the word root are easier for students to recognize as related. For instance, the root *run* sounds the same in *runner* and *running*, whereas the root *heal* does not maintain its sound in the derived words *health* and *healthy*.

- It is easier to recognize a base word (i.e., the special type of word root—a free morpheme) within a derived or inflected word than to recognize a bound root. For instance, *friend* is more recognizable as a meaningful word part in *friendly* than *vis* is in *visible*.

- Words that are derived or inflected forms of common words are more likely to be understood than words that are derived from rarer words. For instance, it is easier to induce the meaning of the words *redo* and *slowly* than *recap* and *succinctly* because *do* and *slow* are more familiar words (and, therefore, more likely known) than *cap* (for *capitulate*) and *succinct*.

Notice that if you did not know what free morphemes, bound morphemes, word roots, derived words, and inflected words were, these findings would mean little to you. We are glad you did not skip the first part of this chapter!

What are the implications of these findings? First, teachers of even young students should alert them to different forms of words, beginning with inflected forms (e.g., plurals, different tenses of verbs, and comparisons). Second, when sharing more complex word forms (beginning in the middle elementary years), such as those with prefixes and derivational suffixes, teachers should start with derived words that maintain the spelling and pronunciation of the word root. Later, teachers should directly teach the relationship between word roots and their derived forms that do not maintain the spelling or pronunciation of the root. Third, teachers will need to explicitly draw students' attention to and teach word roots that are not base words (e.g., *jud* in *prejudice*). Fourth, instruction of derived and inflected forms of word roots should begin with words the students know—that is, common rather than rare words. Fifth, instruction in morphology should occur at every grade level.

In addition, we, like Baumann et al. (2005), recommend that educators teach morphemes in family groups, where they exist. We mean two things by this. One is the more obvious: Teach roots alongside their other forms. For instance, the following words are in the same family in that they share a root (listed first): *play, played, playing, playful, unplayful, playable*. A second type of family is a family of morphemes that have similar meanings. For instance, the following suffixes change a root so as to signify a person: *-er* (as in *reader, writer*, and *composer*), *-ist* (as in *pianist, scientist*, and *artist*), and *-ian* (as in *musician, magician*, and *mathematician*). Thus, as appropriate, these suffixes should be taught together. Similarly, each of the following prefixes can mean "not": *un-* (as in *unable* and *unfriendly*), *il-* (as in *illegal* and *illegible*), *in-* (as in *invisible* and *inedible*), *ir-* (as in *irreplaceable* and *irresistible*), *dis-* (as in *dislike* and *disloyal*), and *non-* (as in *nonstop* and *nonfiction*). Other families include prefixes that signify number, such as *uni-, mono-, bi-, tri-, quad-*, and so forth, and prefixes that signify position, such as *pre-, fore-, mid-, inter-*, and *post-*.

We need to make some final comments here about instruction. Students need to be taught to use morphemic analysis to infer meaning. They need to learn to recognize the components of words and to understand what those components mean. However, most instructional time and energy related to morphology should be devoted to word roots because, as we noted earlier, roots are the heart of words; they carry the meaning that is modified by the addition of affixes. Instruction in affixes—prefixes and suffixes—should focus on those most frequently used, and less time needs to be devoted to inflectional endings, which are learned rather early and easily. Furthermore, morphology is best taught within a context so that its value is obvious. For instance, Greek and Latin had their greatest influence on the language of the sciences. Thus, attention to these roots makes sense not only within the context of language arts instruction but also within the context of content-area instruction.

As a side note, it is interesting to consider the fact that morphemes tend to be spelled consistently (Templeton 2004). Notice, for example, that the written word *sign* includes the letter *g* even though the sound is not heard in the spoken word. The *g* is there because the word *sign* is related to the words *signature, signify*, and *signal*. Thus, the letter *g* is a visual cue to the meaningful relationships among these words. Likewise, think about the spelling of *cleanliness*. Why isn't this word spelled *clenliness*? The answer is that the spelling of the morpheme *clean* is retained in its derived words. What does this mean? It means that teaching students about morphemes supports not only vocabulary development—it also supports spelling development. Furthermore, it helps students discover that our written language has a logic beyond sound-symbol correspondences. What may appear at times arbitrary in terms of phonemes is logical in terms of morphemes. This is a topic for another book!

# Strategies for Teaching Morphemic Analysis

The strategies we suggest center on helping students identify the morphemic units in words and learn their meanings.

### 1. Cut, Mix, and Match

To help students notice word parts, the teacher writes compound words on cards. The cards are given to students, who are encouraged to cut apart the compound words. For instance, given a card with the word *sunshine*, students cut the compound into its two free morphemes so that they now have two cards: one with the word *sun* and one with the word *shine*. Students may then reassemble the cards to create new compound words. A set of cards might include the following compound words: *sailboat, lighthouse, tablecloth, airplane, sunshine, manhunt, yearlong*. When cut apart, the students have these words: *sail, boat, light, house, table, cloth, air, plane, sun, shine, man, hunt, year, long*. The following compounds, then, might be assembled from the pool of words: *houseboat, sailplane, sunlight, boatman, boathouse, airman*.

Students may also create original compound words and illustrate them. Using words from the example, students might construct the compound *airhouse* and draw a picture of a house hovering in the air. As they manipulate meaningful components of language, students gain an understanding of how words are generated and become more observant of word parts.

2. **Find the Word**

Another strategy for drawing attention to morphemes is to provide students with a list of morphologically complex words and ask them to find the "hidden" word. The list should consist of words that contain base words (i.e., free morphemes, or words that can stand alone). Examples include *cats* (cat), *jumping* (jump), and *played* (play) for younger students and *unforgettable* (forget), *unlucky* (luck), and *misplaced* (place) for older students. Students highlight or circle the base word. Students may also be asked to search their textbooks, independent-reading materials, or their own written work to find morphologically complex words and then record the words and their bases in a word journal.

### 3. Find a Partner

Students are each given a large card on which the teacher has written morphemes, one per card. At the teacher's signal, students circulate around the room and find a student with whom they can make a good match. Students stand in their pairs until all students find a partner, and then they share their matches with the group. For instance, if the teacher is working with compound words, cards might include *sun, shine, moon, light, down, hill, finger, print, flood, light, fog, horn, foot, ball, hair, cut, home, work, out, house, over,* and *eat*. If the teacher is working with Latin word roots and their definitions, cards might include *struct, build, port, carry, spect, see, tract, pull, ped, foot, mis, send, min, little, ject, throw, gress,* and *walk*.

You may wish to have students work in groups of three or four. Perhaps you want students to identify words with a common root, and so you have them find classmates whose words contain the same root. Cards might include *astronomy, astronomer, astronaut, microphone, telephone, phonics, symphony, import, export, portable, transport, visible, vision,* and *supervise*.

Students are likely to find the activity related to this strategy more interesting than drawing lines between words on paper. Further, it gives students the opportunity to talk with one another about their words as they circulate and again as they share their matches with other groups.

### 4. Semantic Maps

Raising students' awareness of the relationships among words assists students as they begin to understand how to unlock their meanings. For some students, it comes as a bit of a surprise that words are related. One of the authors recalls the time her fifth-grade son asked her how to spell *finally*. When he was told that the word is related to *final*, he experienced an "Aha moment" and spelled the word instantly. Many students have used and read two related words such as *final* and *finally*, but they may not have ever explicitly thought about them as relatives. Semantic Maps are useful tools for helping students think about the relationships among words.

Semantic Maps are created by placing one word or word element in a circle in the center of a sheet of paper, chart, or board. Students then brainstorm other words that contain that word or word part. Figure 6.6 shows a Semantic Map for the word *do,* and figure 6.7 shows a Semantic Map for the word *run*.

**FIGURE 6.6  Semantic Map for *do***

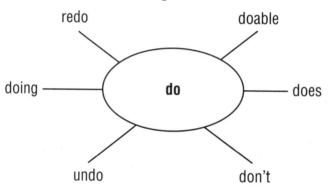

**FIGURE 6.7  Semantic Map for *run***

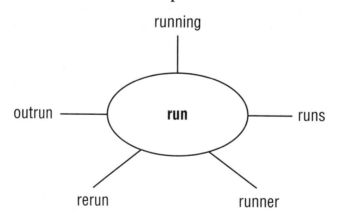

Figure 6.8 shows a Semantic Map for the Latin root *scrib/script*. Surrounding the root are words students recognize as containing the root. Students then discuss how each of their words is related to the meaning of *scrib/script*. A *manuscript* is a written document; to *transcribe* is to make a written copy; a *prescription* is a written order for medicine, and so on.

**FIGURE 6.8 Semantic Map for *scrib/script***

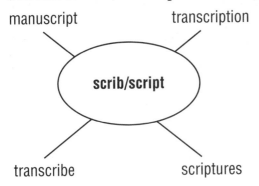

manuscript

transcription

scrib/script

transcribe

scriptures

5. **What's My Rule?**

In this strategy, students examine words to try to determine the rule the teacher is using to sort them. After identifying a word element he or she wants the students to learn, the teacher records sample words such as those listed in figure 6.9 on cards large enough to be seen by the entire class from the front of the room. The teacher gives a word card, perhaps *undecided*, to a student, says the word, and tells the student that the word belongs on the north side of the room (pick any location). The student moves to that location in the room and holds the card for his or her classmates to see. The teacher gives another student the word card *uncle* and says, "This card belongs on the south side of the room." The student moves to the side of the room opposite from where the first student is standing.

The teacher distributes several more word cards, pronounces the words for the students, and tells each student on which side of the room to stand. The teacher does not share his or her rule for sorting the words. After several examples, the teacher shows the next card and asks the students to confer with a neighbor and point to the side of the room where they think the word belongs. The teacher then invites explanations for their decisions and asks for hypotheses about his or her rule, providing a few more examples as necessary. He or she guides the students to the conclusion that the words on the north side of the room all use *un-* as a prefix. The words on the other side of the room start with the letters *un*, but the letters do not function as a prefix in those words. The remainder of the cards are distributed, and the students holding them move to the appropriate sides of the room.

**FIGURE 6.9  Words that begin with *un-***

| Un- Used as a Prefix | Un- Not Used as a Prefix |
| --- | --- |
| undecided | uncle |
| unavoidable | until |
| unhappy | understand |
| unfriendly | underwater |
| unafraid | union |
| unclean | United States |
| unwise | under |
| unwilling | unit |
| unfortunately | unique |

To develop students' understanding of the two meanings of the prefix *un-*, the teacher might use the words listed in figure 6.10. Again, the teacher tells the students holding cards on which side of the room to stand. The teacher's rule is that when *un-* is used to mean "not," the students stand on the right. When *un-* indicates the reversal of an action, the students stand on the left. Students carefully study the words to determine the two meanings of the prefix.

**FIGURE 6.10  Two meanings of the prefix *un-***

| Not | Reversal of an Action |
|---|---|
| unfair | unbend |
| unbroken | untie |
| uncertain | uncap |
| unbelievable | unbutton |
| unaware | unlock |
| unbeaten | unroll |
| uneven | |
| unfamiliar | |
| unexpected | |

Concept-attainment lessons such as these guide students to carefully examine words to determine what they have in common and how they differ. Students think about word structure and word meanings and develop new hypotheses with each additional piece of information until they have enough information to draw an accurate conclusion. It is important for students to see all the words that have been sorted so they can revise their thinking as the lesson progresses. An alternative to having students hold the cards is to use tape or magnets to post them on the board in the front of the room.

6. **Word Sorts**

   We described word sorts in Chapter 5 as a way to reinforce and extend understanding of target words. Sorts are also useful for helping students think about word parts. Here we describe an open sort, one in which the students are free to sort words according to any criterion they choose. The students, and not the teacher, determine the basis for the initial sorting of the words. Ultimately, however, the conversation revolves around the morphemes that are obvious elements of the words the teacher selected.

We provided third-grade students working in pairs with the following words written on cards: *unhappy, refold, unfriendly, rewrite, misplace, unknown, redo, unafraid, mislead, unkind, redraw, reheat, unbeaten, uncover, rearrange, misread,* and *mislay*. Students were given no instructions other than to sort the words in whatever manner made sense to them and that they could explain to their classmates. There were no limits on the number of groupings; students could sort the words into two piles, three piles, or more.

Not surprisingly, most student pairs sorted the words based on the prefix. Words beginning with *un-* were put in one pile, words beginning with *mis-* in another, and words beginning with *re-* were placed in a third pile. Each student pair explained the rule for their sort, and those who did not sort by prefix were acknowledged and then asked to change their groupings so we could all think about the prefixes. We asked the students to talk to their partners about what each of the words in the *re-* group meant. We heard comments such as, "*Refold* means that you fold something again," and "*Redraw* means that you draw something again." After a few moments of partner talk, we asked for whole-group sharing. Students again articulated the meanings of the words. Then we asked, "What do you think *re-* means, given the definitions of all these words?" Students readily commented that *re-* means "again."

Older students may be given words that contain two or three different roots, such as *spectacles, spectator, inspector, inspection, audible, audience, auditorium, audiovisual, dictator, dictate, dictionary, predict,* and *contradict*. Students complete open sorts, discuss their sorts, try alternative sorts, and then sort by word roots. They explain each word's meaning to their partners and to the whole group and then reach conclusions about what the roots mean. Students may consult a dictionary to determine the meanings of some of the words. After discovering what the various roots mean, students try to identify other words that contain the same roots and explain their meanings to the group.

7. **Word Hunts**

Word hunts involve scanning the environment for word parts. After instruction is provided on prefixes, for example, the teacher directs the students to search through books they are currently reading for SSR, their content-area texts, and other print in the classroom (e.g., maps and bulletin board displays) for words with prefixes. Students record the words they find, along with the sources, and then share them with their peers.

Teachers might conduct a small action-research project with their students. After the students search for a given period of time, perhaps 10 minutes, and record each word they find on sticky notes, they aggregate their data by posting those words with like prefixes in the same column on a piece of chart paper. Duplicate words are acceptable. The words in each column are counted, and students discover which prefixes are most common in the sources they perused. The teacher may then wish to share the findings of the White et al. (1989) study we described earlier.

8. **Graffiti Boards**

Similar to word hunts, graffiti boards provide an opportunity for students to share words that contain a given morphemic unit. Students record the words on a piece of chart paper posted in an accessible location in the classroom. In this strategy, students are asked to write words that contain the element any time they have a free moment. For example, the teacher might have an *-ly* chart on display. Students record words they think of or find that contain this element (e.g., *slowly* and *happily*). Periodically, the teacher draws attention to the graffiti board and discusses the students' contributions.

9. **Go Fish**

Go Fish is based on the popular card game. The teacher prepares 52 word cards (about the size of cards in a deck of cards) so there are 13 different sets of four related cards. The four related cards consist of one word root and three derived words (e.g., *struc, structure, construct,* and *destruction* make up one set and *spect, inspect, spectator,* and *spectacle* make up another set). The object of the card game is to collect the most sets of four.

The students form groups of three to six players. Cards are shuffled and five are dealt to each player. The remaining cards are placed facedown in a pile. The player to the dealer's left examines his or her cards. If the student has a set of four, he or she places them faceup. Then the student asks another player of his or her choice for cards in a particular set. For example, the student can say, "LaToya, do you have any words in the *struct* family?" If LaToya does, she hands over all her cards that meet this criterion. If not, LaToya says, "Go Fish," and the player selects a card from the deck. This completes the player's turn, and play moves to the next student. When a player has no more cards, he or she may take one from the deck when it is his or her turn. After all cards are drawn from the deck, however, he or she is out of the game. Play continues until all sets have been played. The winner is the player with the most sets.

Card decks may consist of words that focus on any morphemic unit, including the following:

- Prefixes (e.g., *submarine, subsoil, substandard,* and the definition of *sub-: below or beneath*)

- Suffixes (e.g., *thankful, grateful, spiteful,* and the definition of *-ful: full of*)

- Morphemes in compound words (e.g., *raincoat, rainfall, rainforest,* and *rainspout*)

- Base words (e.g., *love, unloved, lovely,* and *loveable*)

- Latin or Greek roots (e.g., *dictate, dictator, contradict,* and the definition of *dict: to tell*)

## 10. Concentration

Concentration is a game for two to four students that is played with a deck of 30 to 40 word cards that can be paired based on a morpheme. For instance, if the teacher is focusing on prefixes, cards may include *unkind/unhappy, misread/misplaced, preview/predict, review/reorganize,* and so on. If the teacher is focusing on Latin roots, pairs such as *import/export, contract/attract, auditorium/audition* should be prepared. Pairs might also consist of word roots and definitions, such as the following Greek roots and definitions: *aer/air, aster/star, auto/self, derm/skin, hydr/ water, zoo/animal.* One word (or word element) is written on each card. The object of the game is to collect the most pairs of words.

The cards are shuffled and placed facedown in columns and rows. The first player turns two cards faceup. If the cards match (i.e., they both have the same prefix or the same root—whatever the target is), the player keeps both cards and plays again. The player continues until the two upturned cards do not form a pair. These two cards are turned facedown again, and play goes to the student on the player's left. Play continues until all cards have been paired. The winner is the player with the most pairs.

## 11. *Jeopardy!*®

Bear et al. (2004) share a modification of the popular television show *Jeopardy!*. A *Jeopardy!* board is displayed (perhaps cards in a pocket chart) and items worth 100 to 500 points are posted in each of several categories. For example, in *Jeopardy!* for Latin roots, five roots—*spect, form, port, tract,* and *dict*—make up the categories. When a student selects *port* for 100 points, the teacher or student leader selects the card, looks on the back and reads the hint, which in *Jeopardy!* is stated as an answer. The player provides the vocabulary term in the form of a question. Thus, given the clue in the *port* category, "Someone who carries baggage," the player responds, "What is a *porter*?" to earn 100 points.

After students are introduced to the game, they may create their own *Jeopardy!* questions and answers and write them on index cards. Point values are written on one side; the question and answer are written on the other.

## Morphology and English Language Learners

Not long ago, the son of one of the authors came across the word *facilitated*. Peter commented that the word was easy. He said he knew what it meant because the word is very much like a common Spanish word he learned in school: *fácil*. He used his knowledge in one language to help him understand a word in a different language. Peter recognized the link between the languages and broadened his vocabulary as a result!

One of the benefits of teaching morphology is that students begin to look closely at words, and with teacher guidance, they develop eyes and ears that notice similarities in words across languages. Cognates (from the Latin word meaning "born together") are words in different languages that have the same origin. For instance, the Romance languages (e.g., French, Portuguese, Italian, and Spanish) have their roots in Latin. Many English words have Latin roots as well. (When the Normans conquered England, Latin-based French words were added to the Germanic-based vocabulary of the Anglo-Saxons.) Given their shared past, many of these words today are similar in pronunciation, spelling, and meaning. Including instruction in cognates, particularly as students explore word parts, then, is a powerful way to support language growth of English language learners. We might add here that some words that are similar in pronunciation, spelling, and meaning are not true cognates because they do not have a common origin. Even so, we can take advantage of their similarities.

Think about the following words in English and Spanish. Notice the similar parts in these word pairs: *bicycle/bicicleta, family/familia, generosity/generosidad, globe/globo, line/linea, list/lista, primary/primero, rare/raro, traffic/tráfico, vacant/vacía, significant/significar.* Capitalizing on students' native languages to support their learning of English is empowering and should not be overlooked as we provide vocabulary instruction.

We have a quick and important caution: Some words are what have been called "false cognates" or "false friends." These are words in two languages that are similar in spelling and pronunciation but not in meaning. For example, *bizarre* means "peculiar" in English, whereas *bizarro* means "courageous" or "generous" in Spanish. You would not want to think you were complimenting someone when in fact you were insulting him or her! Similarly, you do not want to say you are *embarazada* if you are *embarrassed*, or that you are *embarrassed* if you are *embarazada* because the Spanish word means "pregnant"!

Looking within words for clues to meaning is an important strategy for all language learners. Students should ask themselves: Can my knowledge of parts of a particular word help me understand the meaning of the whole word? We turn now from this *intraword* (*intra* is derived from the Latin word meaning "within") word-learning strategy to an *interword* (*inter* is from the Latin word meaning "between" or "among") strategy: contextual analysis.

# Learning Word Meanings from Context

Because much of students' exposure to new words occurs as they read, making use of the context to understand unknown words is an essential word-learning strategy. Furthermore, the use of context will be helpful to students who look at word parts to infer word meanings. After students think they understand a word based on its parts, they need to consider the context in which they found the word. Does their inference make sense given the context?

Teachers must guide students to understand that if they are to figure out the meaning of a word, they need to examine the subtle and not-so-subtle hints and clues the author provides. That is, they must consider more than the word itself; they must also consider the context in which it is used to determine its meaning. Students come to realize that this is not a perfect process but, like the game of horseshoes, they can often come close enough to ascertain a word's meaning. Importantly, students will be most motivated to use context clues when they have personally valuable reasons for understanding a word. We are all most apt to want to know the meanings of words in material that excites, interests, or educates us. Asking students to read *Neurological Pathways of the South American Tapeworm* when one of Lemony Snicket's *Unfortunate Events* books (Harper Collins) resides in their desks often will result in new tapeworm vocabulary being glossed over or ignored.

Teachers should explain to students that some authors provide a considerable amount of information to support understanding of challenging words, whereas others provide a lean amount of information (Baker, Simmons, and Kame'enui 1998). Further, the types of context clues vary. Although many books offer picture and graphic clues, we focus here on linguistic clues, both syntactic (i.e., word order) and semantic (i.e., meaning). Edwards and her colleagues (2004) identified the following types of linguistic clues: direct definitions, synonyms, examples, contrasts or antonyms, and other sentence- or paragraph-level support.

## Direct definitions

Authors sometimes provide a direct definition of a word, as is the case with the words *meteor* and *weather* in these two sentences:

- A *meteor* is a piece of space dust or rock that burns up as it enters Earth's atmosphere.

- To *weather* a storm means to come safely through it.

The meanings of the words are directly and explicitly provided for readers. Notice the use of the word *is* in the first sentence and *means* in the second sentence. Readers know they are being provided definitions.

Sometimes a writer uses a comma to signal a definition or includes words such as *or, that is*, and *in other words,* as in the following:

- We are still on the *frontside* of the moon, the quarters that lead up to the full moon.

- *Apparitions,* or ghostly figures, often make scary stories especially frightening.

## Synonyms

Authors sometimes use a synonym near an unfamiliar word, as in these sentences:

- I was the *penultimate* person in a very long line. Being next to last was discouraging.

- I was warned she was *loquacious*, and she was indeed the most talkative person I have ever met.

The phrase *next to last* in the first sentence and the word *talkative* in the second sentence clarify the meanings of the italicized words.

## Examples

The use of examples also may provide clues to a word's meaning. Notice how the examples facilitate understanding of the word *onomatopoeia*:

- Students often enjoy *onomatopoeia* and use words such as *buzz, cuckoo, boom, zip, clang,* and *swish* in their writing.

## Contrast or antonyms

Meanings of unknown words are sometimes revealed through the use of contrasts or antonyms. Hints such as *instead of, unlike, rather than,* and *opposed to* are helpful, as in this sentence:

- Unlike his talkative brother, Eduardo was *taciturn* by nature.

## Other context clues

Sometimes the immediate sentence will not provide sufficient contextual information for students to determine the meaning of an unfamiliar word. For example, the italicized word in this sentence cannot be understood by using the immediate context:

- His stomach was *lavaged*.

However, when read in a larger context, the meaning of the word becomes apparent.

- He accidentally picked up the wrong container and swallowed a substantial amount of the poison. Acting quickly, his family called the paramedics. They transported him to the hospital where the ER physicians inserted a long tube down his throat. His stomach was *lavaged*. His life was saved.

Do you understand the word *lavage* when given this larger context? To *lavage* is to wash out a hollow body organ, such as a stomach, using a flow of water or saline. Sometimes we say an individual has had his or her "stomach pumped." Insufficient information is provided in the sentence to help us understand the word, whereas considerable information is provided in the paragraph.

Bishop and Bishop stated, "It must be stressed that the use of context moves well beyond the sentence level. When students have a firm understanding of the book they are reading, they have created a context and know every word they encounter should fit within the context" (1996, 68). Sometimes the clue to the word meaning is available even before the selection is read. For instance, when a scary book is selected, the reader is aware that there will be an abundance of scary words encountered, as in this example:

- Hector turned the corner only to see the *apparition* appear immediately in front of him. Hector's hair stood on end and goose bumps ran up and down his arms. Was this creature the same one who had come right through George's closed door? That Hector could see right through it did nothing to quell his fear.

Providing reasons for reading and engaging students in thinking about the content of a selection prior to reading can facilitate students' abilities to use context to understand unknown words.

## Strategies for Teaching Use of Context

Graves and Watts-Taffe stated that the most widely recommended and most useful word-learning strategy is using context. They asserted that "carefully planned and robust instruction in using context clues should be part of a comprehensive vocabulary program" (2002, 143–144). Greenwood and Flanigan (2007) agreed, noting that because context clues are very transportable, they merit careful teaching. Although others argue that context is often unhelpful or even misleading (Beck, McKeown, and Kucan 2002), sufficient research suggests that instruction in the use of context to derive word meanings is worthwhile (Fukkink and De Glopper 1998).

In general, we recommend the following:

- In both oral and written language interactions, emphasis should be on meaning. As a result, students will know that individual words contribute to meaning. Students will anticipate that something relevant and logical is intended by the use of an unknown word. They will be thinkers and approach language interactions as meaning makers. This recommendation is especially important for teachers of English language learners.

- Contextual analysis should be taught explicitly; teachers should familiarize students with the variety of clues that authors provide to support meaning, while also reminding students that not all contexts are helpful in determining word meanings.

- Teachers should model the use of context to confront unknown words by thinking aloud. Students need to witness contextual analysis in action in authentic circumstances, such as when the teacher reads aloud.

- Teachers should scaffold students' use of context to build initial hypotheses about the meaning of an unknown word.

In the remainder of this section, we provide several strategies for building students' abilities to use context for word learning. We begin with strategies that draw students' attention to reading as a meaning-making endeavor. These strategies support an understanding of reading as thinking. When students who are thinkers confront a new word in the context of reading, they ask themselves, What might this mean? What would make sense here? Then we share strategies that focus specifically on the kinds of context clues authors use.

### 1. Prereading Discussions

Students are most willing to learn and use a strategy when they see it as helping them accomplish something important. As stated earlier, when students find what they are reading interesting and useful, chances are increased that they will be motivated to use context clues. Similarly, when students have some background knowledge of the content, they will more likely be able to use context clues to determine a word's meaning (Fore, Boon, and Lowrie 2007).

Prereading discussions that pique students' interest and that build or activate background knowledge can set the stage for readers to use context to support their understanding of unfamiliar words. Using an appealing work of literature such as Sendak's *Where the Wild Things Are* (1988), teachers of young students may take two or three minutes to share the book cover, read the title, and discuss what might happen in the story. Through this process, the teacher guides students to develop both a reason for reading the story and predictions about the story. Engaging older students in hands-on lessons, exciting demonstrations, activities that draw on their personal experiences, and strategies that spark conversations about a topic prior to reading guides them to actively approach a text.

2. **The Predictable Pause**

For all students, but especially those in the early grades, having literature read to them is important to using context clues. A simple pause can be highly effective for helping students think about how words make sense in the context of the text. And the strategy helps students view themselves as active participants in the reading process. When reading aloud to students, the teacher simply pauses slightly just before a highly predictable word or phrase. For example, when sharing Viorst's *Alexander and the Terrible, Horrible, No Good, Very Bad Day* (1987), the teacher pauses just before "even in Australia," a phrase that is repeated several times. It is the rare student who can refrain from calling out the phrase. Students' use of context clues develops most readily when they have the language of literacy running through their heads like a familiar song. The same certainly holds true with expository material. The more students hear what informational text material sounds like and the more the tone and structure of such material becomes familiar, the more easily and naturally context clues are used.

3. **Cloze Technique**

   Cloze is a technique in which the reader supplies words that have been deleted from a sentence or passage. In order to make reasonable word suggestions, students must attend to the content and the language surrounding the missing word. What is the topic of the selection? What word would make sense in the general context? What would make sense in the immediate context of the sentence? What kind of word is needed? The following progression might be useful for guiding students to recognize the support that context can provide:

   - Present students with several words from which to select as they determine the deleted word.

   - Present the initial letter or letter combinations for the missing words.

   - Use passages in which highly predictable words are deleted.

   - Use passages in which every fifth word is deleted.

   Teachers should model each step and engage students in conversations about their word choices. Then students may work in groups or pairs to complete cloze sentences. Finally, having been carefully moved toward independence, students work individually. The importance of this strategy is that it gives students insights into the fact that context can contribute to their understanding of words.

4. **Context Clues and Semantic Gradients**

   Greenwood and Flanigan (2007) developed an instructional

technique that combines context clues with semantic gradients to enhance students' vocabulary understanding. We described semantic gradients, or linear arrays, in Chapter 5. Semantic gradients are related words placed along a continuum (e.g., *tiny, little, average, big, huge*). Working with semantic gradients helps students recognize shades of meaning.

In this combined strategy, students are provided increasingly more informative cloze sentences. The first sentence allows for many possibilities. Greenwood and Flanigan used the following sentence as an example: "The teacher was _____." Students are then given a word continuum such as *happy, pleased, disappointed, upset*, and *livid*. Students realize that given the context, any of these words will make sense in the sentence. They are then given an enriched version of the same sentence: "The teacher was _____ because the class behaved so well." It contains more information, so the number of reasonable options decreases. A third version of the sentence is provided, one with a different context: "The teacher was _____ because the class was so unruly." New possibilities are discussed. Then an even richer context is provided, and students select the word that makes the most sense. During discussions, the students are guided to understand that context narrows the possibilities. Eventually, students can compose their own semantic gradients and corresponding sentences.

5. **Sorts**

As you may have observed, we have suggested the use of sorts several times in this book. Sorting helps students think about word meanings, notice components of words, or in this case, identify types of context clues. Students must closely examine the items in order to make sorting decisions.

Initially, items for sorting should be simple and straightforward, and the number of categories should be minimal. For example, after students have learned that sometimes an author provides a direct definition of a term (especially in informational texts), students sort cards prepared by the teacher into one of two stacks: sentences in which there is a direct definition of a challenging term and sentences in which there is not a direct definition of a challenging term. Where would you place these sentences?

- To *prettify* means to make pretty.

- An *intersection* is a place where two or more roads meet.

- He *kibbled* the grain.

- She prepared the *kindling* and placed it outside the back door.

Hopefully, you said that the first two sentences belong in a "direct definition provided" stack and the final two sentences belong in a "no direct definition provided" stack.

Later, students can sort based on clue type. For instance, beginning with just two categories, students might sort the following sentence cards into those that provide direct definition clues and those that provide contrast or antonym clues:

- Unlike her willing friend, she was *reluctant* to dive into the water.

- The *prestidigitator*, or sleight-of-hand artist, amused the audience with her card tricks.

- His life was one of *privation*, one lacking in the usual comforts and necessities of life.

- She hoped her future would be one of *affluence* rather than poverty.

- Although normally *affable*, Joan was quiet and reserved around others at the party.

## 6. Clue Hunts

Any strategy is more meaningful when it is used in an authentic context. After students have been taught that authors sometimes provide clues to word meanings, the teacher may encourage them to go on a clue hunt and find examples of context clues in their reading materials. These may be recorded on a class chart and then later sorted into types.

The teacher may wish to begin by having students look in their textbooks as he or she guides students through a page or chapter. Together the students and the teacher examine the author's language for clues. Later, students work in pairs or small groups. Eventually, they independently search texts and share examples.

## 7. Write

Students will understand the power of authors' words and the deliberateness with which they choose their words when students engage in writing. In order to deepen their appreciation of context clues, students can be asked to write sentences or passages in which they provide context clues for target words. What words might they target? Consider the following:

- Students may select words that they find personally challenging or that they believe would be challenging to their classmates.

- The teacher may select specialized content vocabulary from a topic under study in one of the content areas.

- Words and the passages that contain them may be borrowed from a text selection or work of literature. This is especially useful when the passages provide insufficient information for determining meaning. Students rewrite a brief passage that contains a difficult word and make it more understandable for others through context.

# Learning Word Meanings from the Dictionary

One of the authors' husbands is a model of independent word learning. Bert is a voracious reader, and we are certain that he uses both morphemic analysis and contextual analysis to infer the meanings of the unknown words he encounters. The strategy he employs that is most apparent to others, however, is his use of the dictionary. Bert keeps an old dictionary—one that he has had for many years—by his side as he reads. It moves from the bedroom to the home office to the family room, and it is not unusual to see him look up words. Particularly interesting is that Bert also keeps a highlighter handy. He uses it to highlight the words he looks up. If you were to flip through the pages of his worn dictionary, you would see yellow markings sprinkled throughout. You would notice that at some point in time he looked up *beleaguer*. On other occasions, he looked up *truss, cognomen,* and *laudatory*. You would find quite a few yellowed words here and there. What you might also be struck by, particularly since he has been doing this for many years, is that the vast majority of words in his dictionary have not been yellowed. Of course, when you think about it, this makes sense. Many of the words that he reads he either already understands or he figures out on the spot. And some of the unhighlighted words he simply has not encountered in his reading. This, too, is not surprising, given the enormous number of words in the English language.

Bert highlights the words as a way of reminding himself that he has visited them. Sometimes he peruses the dictionary to find highlighted words and review their meanings. Sometimes he looks up an unknown word only to discover that it is highlighted. He has visited it before!

The ability to use the dictionary is another independent word-learning strategy. However, as we noted in Chapter 5, dictionary definitions can sometimes be less than helpful. Nevertheless, we want our students to see the dictionary as a possible aid. Therefore, in this final section, we describe several strategies that inspire students to spend some time with the dictionary.

Our general recommendations include the following:

- Teachers should model dictionary use by looking up interesting or challenging words as the need arises.

- Students must be provided instruction in how to use a dictionary so that it is a helpful tool, not an instrument of agony and annoyance.

- Students should be exposed to a variety of dictionaries, including online dictionaries.

## Strategies for Engaging with Dictionaries

### 1. Fictionary

Fictionary is an entertaining game in which students meet in small groups to talk about words and their definitions. Each group has a dictionary and a stack of blank paper. One student quickly peruses the dictionary to find a word that he or she thinks his or her peers do not know. The student pronounces and spells the word for the group members but does not tell them what it means. Everyone in the group records the word on a piece of paper and attempts to write an official-sounding definition. If someone knows the word's meaning, the student may write it, or he or she may invent a definition to try to trick the student's peers. The student who selected the word from the dictionary writes the correct definition on a sheet of paper. All papers are handed to the student. He or she shuffles them and reads aloud all of the proposed definitions without identifying the authors. Students vote for the definition they think is correct, and then the real definition is revealed. Students who voted for the correct definition are awarded two points, and those whose definition received votes are awarded one point for each vote. Students most familiar with the language of a dictionary are most likely to be able to write definitions that mislead their peers, and so they garner points. The dictionary is passed to the next person in the group and play continues as long as time permits. The student with the most points is the winner.

An alternative version of the game is to ask each student to select one or more words from a dictionary and write the correct definition and two additional incorrect definitions for each. In small groups, the students each share their words and the three definitions. Students vote on which they believe is the accurate definition. The student sharing the word receives a point for every student who votes for an incorrect definition.

2. **Personal Dictionaries**

Unlike Bert, who highlights words in his dictionary, students probably cannot mark in the dictionaries provided by the school. However, they can keep dictionary journals. As a matter of routine, students record words they looked up in a dictionary in their personal dictionary journal. They write the word, note where they came across it (e.g., "in our social studies textbook," "my mother used it," "in the first paragraph of my new library book"), and record its appropriate meaning. At the end of each week, students share in pairs or small groups the words they recorded.

3. **Celebrate Dictionary Day**

Did you know that October 16 is Dictionary Day? It was

named in honor of the birthday of Noah Webster, author of the first American dictionary. Teachers might celebrate the day by having their class create a dictionary of words to help next year's students. Students think about what they have studied to date. They revisit notes, texts, and tests; they list topics and activities. Then they identify important words related to the content and construct a dictionary. Middle and high school students might work in teams organized around units of study. For instance, the science teacher might guide the students to form these teams: tools and measurement in science, the scientific process, properties of matter, and the atom. Elementary school students might work in content teams so that one team is responsible for thinking about important vocabulary in social studies and another team is responsible for thinking about important vocabulary in art. With younger students, the teacher can lead a discussion about what students have learned so far this school year and help them identify and record important words on large sheets of construction paper. With the teacher's guidance and support, students develop definitions, which are also recorded.

Because images are supportive of vocabulary learning, the class dictionary should include illustrations. Binding the final product will add to its importance, and the dictionary should be placed on display so current and future students can refer to it. If time and materials are sufficient, enough copies can be made to give each of next year's students their own personal copy.

# Conclusion

Instruction in word-learning strategies is an important aspect of a multifaceted vocabulary program. Students can be taught to look within words for clues to their meanings; teaching morphemes and morphemic analysis increases students' understanding of words exponentially. Students also can be taught to look outside an unfamiliar word to the context in which they encounter it.

What is the big picture? What does the reader already know? What linguistic clues has the author provided that support understanding of the word? And students can be taught to look beyond the word and its context to an important resource—the dictionary. These word-learning strategies empower students to independently learn new words.

# Think About It!

1. Read the passage below and insert words where they have been omitted. Then talk with others about whether you found the task easy or difficult. If you had been asked to complete the passage prior to reading the chapter, would your experience have been the same?

   Building students' independent word-learning _____ is an important responsibility of teachers. These strategies include _____ analysis. Students are taught to recognize morphemes, the smallest units of _____ in a word. Morphemes include roots, _____, and suffixes. A second word-learning strategy is contextual _____. Teachers guide students to think beyond the _____ to the context in which it is encountered. Authors sometimes provide context _____ that help readers understand unknown words. Finally, teachers can support students' use of the _____, an important resource.

2. Look through one of your texts and identify morphologically complex words. How will you teach these words?

3. Think about your vocabulary program. How do you or might you address independence in vocabulary learning in every content area?

# Final Words

———— •—•—•— ————

*"Vocabulary enables us to interpret and to express. If you have a limited vocabulary, you will also have a limited vision and a limited future."*

—Jim Rohn

———— •—•—•— ————

We teach so that our students have the ability and desire to make the world a better place. To do so, they must have the skills, knowledge, and values necessary to successfully assume this responsibility. Vocabulary knowledge and the skills to acquire new vocabulary are essential components of the education we provide to our students. Vocabulary enhances comprehension, and comprehension—with appropriate instruction—leads to critical thinking. Critical thinking results in the making of informed decisions, the kind of decisions that provide students with the desire and ability to contribute to society in positive and productive ways. We hope we have made the case for vocabulary's importance and that *Vocabulary Instruction for Academic Success* has provided an abundance of instructional strategies that can be used in your classroom or educational setting. Along the way, we certainly enriched our own vocabularies and hope we have enriched yours.

As we close, we would like to identify 10 important words from this book (a strategy described in Chapter 4). Because there are three of us, we will share 30 words. We invite you to think about our words; why we selected them; how we used them in the book;

and how they might be sorted, organized, or linked together. We urge you to compare them to the words from this book that you would have selected. For us, the words below convey profoundly important ideas, and we hope they do for you as well.

| | | |
|---|---|---|
| vocabulary | experience | language input |
| comprehension | exposure | language output |
| academic vocabulary | repetition | intentional |
| success | context | opportunities |
| knowledge | relationships | read |
| interactions | active | rare |
| gap | variety | friendly explanations |
| complex | morphemic analysis | sorts |
| instruction | dictionaries | writing |
| multifaceted | curriculum | word-learning strategies |

# References Cited

Akhtar, N., J. Jipson, and M. A. Callanan. 2001. Learning words through overhearing. *Child Development* 72 (2): 416–30.

Anderson, R. C., P. T. Wilson, and L. G. Fielding. 1988. Growth in reading and how children spend their time outside of school. *Reading Research Quarterly* 23 (3): 285–303.

Applegate, A. J., and M. D. Applegate. 2004. The Peter effect: Reading habits and attitudes of preservice teachers. *The Reading Teacher* 57 (6): 554–63.

Ashton-Warner, S. 1963. *Teacher*. New York: Simon & Schuster.

Ayto, J. 1993. *Dictionary of word origins*. New York: Arcade Publishing.

Bailey, A. L. 2007. Introduction. In *The language demands of school: Putting academic English to the test*, ed. A. L. Bailey, 1–26. New Haven, CT: Yale University Press.

Baker, S. K., D. C. Simmons, and E. J. Kame'enui. 1998. Vocabulary acquisition: Instructional and curricular basics and implications. In *What reading research tells us about children with diverse learning needs: Bases and basics*, ed. D. C. Simmons and E. J. Kame'enui, 219–38. Mahwah, NJ: Lawrence Erlbaum.

Baumann, J. F., E. C. Edwards, E. M. Boland, S. Olejnik, and E. J. Kame'enui. 2003. Vocabulary tricks: Effects of instruction in morphology and context on fifth-grade students' ability to derive and infer word meanings. *American Educational Research Journal* 40 (2): 447–94.

Baumann, J. F., G. Font, E. C. Edwards, and E. Boland. 2005. Strategies for teaching middle-grade students to use word-part and context clues to expand reading vocabulary. In *Teaching and learning vocabulary: Bringing research to practice*, ed. E. H. Hiebert and M. L. Kamil, 179–205. Mahwah, NJ: Lawrence Erlbaum.

Baumann, J. F., E. J. Kame'enui, and G. E. Ash. 2003. Research on vocabulary instruction: Voltaire redux. In *Handbook of research on teaching the English language arts*, ed. J. Flood, D. Lapp, J. Squire, and J. Jensen, 752–85. Mahwah, NJ: Lawrence Erlbaum.

Bear, D. R., M. Invernizzi, S. Templeton, and F. Johnston. 2004. *Words their way: Word study for phonics, vocabulary, and spelling instruction*. 3rd ed. Upper Saddle River, NJ: Pearson.

Beck, I. L., and M. G. McKeown. 2001. Text talk: Capturing the benefits of read-aloud experiences for young children. *The Reading Teacher* 55 (1): 10–20.

Beck, I. L., M. G. McKeown, and L. Kucan. 2002. *Bringing words to life: Robust vocabulary instruction*. New York: Guilford.

Bishop, A., and S. Bishop. 1996. *Teaching phonics, phonemic awareness, and word recognition*. Westminster, CA: Teacher Created Materials.

Blachowicz, C., and P. J. Fisher. 2005. *Teaching vocabulary in all classrooms*. 3rd ed. Upper Saddle River, NJ: Merrill.

Blachowicz, C., P. J. Fisher, D. Ogle, and S. Watts-Taffe. 2006. Vocabulary: Questions from the classroom. *Reading Research Quarterly* 41 (4): 524–39.

Brechtel, M. 2001. *Bringing it all together*. Carlsbad, CA: Dominie.

Carroll, J. B., P. Davies, and B. Richman. 1971. *The American heritage word frequency book*. Boston: Houghton Mifflin.

Cassidy, J., and D. Cassidy. 2008. What's hot, what's not for 2008. *Reading Today* 25 (4): 1, 10–11.

Cazden, C. 1986. Classroom discourse. In *Handbook of research on teaching*, ed. M. Wittrock, 432–63. New York: Macmillan.

Collins, M. F. 2005. ESL preschoolers' English vocabulary acquisition from storybook reading. *Reading Research Quarterly* 40 (4): 406–8.

Cunningham, A. E. 2005. Vocabulary growth through independent reading and reading aloud to children. In *Teaching and learning vocabulary: Bringing research to practice*, ed. E. H. Hiebert and M. L. Kamil, 45–68. Mahwah, NJ: Lawrence Erlbaum.

Cunningham, A. E., and K. E. Stanovich. 1991. Tracking the unique effects of print exposure in children: Associations with vocabulary, general knowledge, and spelling. *Journal of Educational Psychology* 83 (2): 264–74.

———. 2003. Reading matters: How reading engagement influences cognition. In *Handbook of research on teaching the English language arts*, ed. J. Flood, D. Lapp, J.R. Squire, and J.M. Jensen, 666–75. Mahwah, NJ: Lawrence Erlbaum.

Daniels, H. 1994. *Literature circles: Voice and choice in the student-centered classroom.* Portland, ME: Stenhouse.

Day, H. I. 1982. Curiosity and the interested explorer. *Performance and Instruction*, 21 (4): 19–22.

*DK dictionary.* 1997. London: Dorling Kindersley.

Dreher, M. J. 2003. Motivating teachers to read. *The Reading Teacher* 56 (4): 338–40.

Duke, N. 2000. 3.6 minutes per day: The scarcity of informational texts in first grade. *Reading Research Quarterly* 35 (2): 202–24.

Dunlap, C. Z., and E. M. Weisman. 2006. *Helping English language learners succeed.* Huntington Beach, CA: Shell Education.

Edwards, E. C., G. Font, J. F. Baumann, and E. Boland. 2004. Unlocking word meanings: Strategies and guidelines for teaching morphemic and contextual analysis. In *Vocabulary instruction: Research to practice*, ed. J. F. Baumann and E. J. Kame'enui, 159–76. New York: Guilford Press.

Fisher, P., and C. Blachowicz. 2007. Teaching how to think about words. *Voices in the middle* 15 (1): 6–12.

Fore III, C., R. T. Boon, and K. Lowrie. 2007. Vocabulary instruction for middle school students with learning disabilities: A comparison of two instructional models. *Learning Disabilities: A Contemporary Journal* 5 (2): 49–73.

Frayer, D., W. C. Frederick, and H. J. Klausmeier. 1969. *A schema for testing the level of cognitive mastery.* Madison, WI: Wisconsin Center for Education Research.

Fukkink, R. G., and K. De Glopper. 1998. Effects of instruction in deriving word meaning from context: A meta-analysis. *Review of Educational Research* 68 (4): 450–69.

Funk, C. E., and D. E. Funk, Jr. 1986. *Horsefeathers and other curious words*. New York: Harper Collins.

Gambrell, L. B. 1996. Creating classroom cultures that foster reading motivation. *The Reading Teacher* 50 (1): 14–25.

———. 2007. Promoting pleasure reading: The role of models, mentors, and motivators. *Reading Today* 25 (1): 16.

Graves, M. F., and S. M. Watts-Taffe. 2002. The place of word consciousness in a research-based vocabulary program. In *What research has to say about reading instruction*, ed. A. E. Farstrup and S. J. Samuels, 140–65. Newark, DE: International Reading Association.

Greenwood, S. C., and K. Flanigan. 2007. Overlapping vocabulary and comprehension: Context clues complement semantic gradients. *The Reading Teacher* 61 (3): 249–54.

Guillaume, A. M., R. H. Yopp, and H. K. Yopp. 2007. *50 strategies for active teaching: Engaging K-12 learners in the classroom*. Upper Saddle River, NJ: Pearson.

Guthrie, J. T., and A. Wiggins. 2000. Engagement and motivation in reading. In *Handbook of reading research: Volume III*, ed. M.L. Kamil, P. B. Mosenthal, P.D. Pearson, and R. Barr 403–22. Mahwah, NJ: Lawrence Erlbaum.

Haggard, M. R. 1982. The vocabulary self-collection strategy: An active approach to word learning. *Journal of Reading* 26 (3): 203–7.

Harste, J. C., K. G. Short, and C. Burke. 1988. *Creating classrooms for authors: The reading writing connection*. Portsmouth, NH: Heinemann.

Hart, B., and T. R. Risley. 1995. *Meaningful differences in the everyday experience of young American children*. Baltimore, MD: Paul H. Brookes.

———. 2003. The early catastrophe: The 30 million word gap by age 3. *American Educator* 27 (1): 4–9.

Hayes, D. P., and M. Ahrens. 1988. Vocabulary simplification for children: A special case of 'motherese'? *Journal of Child Language* 15 (2): 395–410.

Hefflin, B. R., and M. A. Barksdale-Ladd. 2001. African American children's literature that helps students find themselves: Selection guidelines for grades K–3. *The Reading Teacher* 54 (8): 810–19.

Heritage, M., N. Silva, and M. Pierce. 2007. Academic English: A view from the classroom. In *The language demands of school: Putting academic English to the test*, ed. A. L. Bailey, 171–210. New Haven, NJ: Yale University Press.

Hiebert, E. H. 2005. In pursuit of an effective, efficient vocabulary curriculum for the elementary grades. In *Teaching and learning vocabulary: Bringing research to practice*, ed. E. H. Hiebert and M. L. Kamil, 243–63. Mahwah, NJ: Lawrence Erlbaum.

Hirsch, Jr., E. D. 2003. Reading comprehension requires knowledge— of words and the world. *American Educator* (Spring): 10–22, 28–29, 44–45.

Huttenlocher, J., M. Vasilyeva, E. Cymerman, and S. Levine. 2002. Language input and child syntax. *Cognitive Psychology* 45 (3): 337– 74.

Johnson, D. 2001. *Vocabulary in the elementary and middle school*. Boston: Allyn and Bacon.

Kagan, S. 1994. *Cooperative learning*. San Clemente, CA: Kagan Cooperative.

Kamil, M. L., and E. H. Hiebert. 2005. Teaching and learning vocabulary: Perspectives and persistent issues. In *Teaching and learning vocabulary: Bringing research to practice*, ed. E. H. Hiebert and M.L. Kamil, 1–23

Kieffer, M. J., and N. K. Lesaux. 2007. Breaking down words to build meaning: Morphology, vocabulary, and reading comprehension in the urban classroom. *The Reading Teacher* 61 (2): 134–44.

Kuo, L., and R. C. Anderson. 2006. Morphological awareness and learning to read: A cross-language perspective. *Educational Psychologist* 41 (3): 161–80.

Lehr, F., J. Osborn, and E. H. Hiebert. 2004. *A focus on vocabulary*. Honolulu, HI: Pacific Resources for Education and Learning.

Lyman, F. 1981. The responsive classroom discussion: The inclusion of all students. In *Mainstreaming digest*, ed. A. S. Anderson, 109–13. College Park, MD: University of Maryland Press.

Marzano, R. J. 2004. *Building background knowledge for academic achievement: Research on what works in schools*. Alexandria, VA: Association for Supervision and Curriculum Development.

McBride-Chang, C., R. K. Wagner, A. Muse, B. W. Y. Chow, and H. Shu. 2005. The role of morphological awareness in children's vocabulary acquisition in English. *Applied Psycholinguistics* 26 (3): 415–35.

McKeown, M. G. 1993. Creating effective definitions for young word learners. *Reading Research Quarterly* 28 (1): 16–31.

*Merriam-Webster new book of word histories*. 1991. Springfield, MA: Merriam-Webster.

Miller, G. A., and P. M. Gildea. 1985. *How to misread a dictionary*. AILA Bulletin. 13–26. Pisa: AILA (International Association for Applied Linguistics).

Nagy, W. 2005. Why vocabulary instruction needs to be long-term and comprehensive. In *Teaching and learning vocabulary: Bringing research to practice*, ed. E. H. Hiebert and M. L. Kamil, 27–44. Mahwah, NJ: Lawrence Erlbaum.

———. 2006. *Five things teachers need to know about words and word learning*. Presentation at the annual meeting of the National Reading Conference, Los Angeles.

Nagy, W. E., and P. A. Herman. 1987. Breadth and depth of vocabulary knowledge: Implications for acquisition and instruction. In *The nature of vocabulary acquisition*, ed. M. G. McKeown and M. E. Curtis, 19–35. Mahwah, NJ: Lawrence Erlbaum.

Nagy, W., and J. A. Scott. 2000. Vocabulary processes. In vol. 3 of *Handbook of reading research*, ed. M. L. Kamil, P. B. Mosenthal, P. D. Pearson, and R. Barr, 269–84. Mahwah, NJ: Lawrence Erlbaum.

Nagy, W., V. W. Berninger, and R. D. Abbott. 2006. Contributions of morphology beyond phonology to literacy outcomes of upper elementary and middle-school students. *Journal of Educational Psychology* 98 (1): 134–47.

National Center for Education Statistics. 2003. Highlights from the TIMSS 1999 video study of eighth-grade mathematics teaching. Retrieved March 26, 2006, from http://nces.ed.gov/pubs2003/timssvideo/2.asp

National Institute of Child Health and Human Development. 2000. *Teaching children to read: An evidence-based assessment of the scientific research literature on reading and its implications for reading instruction*. Report of the National Reading Panel. Washington, DC: U.S. Government Print Office.

Ogle, D. 1986. K-W-L: A teaching model that develops active reading of expository text. *The Reading Teacher* 39 (6): 564–70.

Paivio, A. 1990. *Mental representation: A dual coding approach*. New York: Oxford University Press.

Palmer, B. M., R. M. Codling, and L. B. Gambrell. 1994. In their own words: What elementary students have to say about motivation to read. *The Reading Teacher* 48 (2): 176–78.

Pinnell, G. S., and A. M. Jaggar. 2003. Oral language: Speaking and listening in elementary classrooms. In *Handbook of research on teaching the English language arts*, ed. J. Flood, D. Lapp, J. R. Squire, and J. M Jensen, 881–913. Mahwah, NJ: Lawrence Erlbaum.

Powell, W. R. 1986. Teaching vocabulary through opposition. *Journal of Reading* 29 (7): 617–21.

Pressley, M., and K. Hilden. 2002. How can children be taught to comprehend text better? In *Successful reading instruction: Research in educational productivity*, ed. M. L. Kamil, J. B. Manning, and H. J. Walberg, 33–51. Greenwich, CT: Information Age Publishing.

Ruddell, M. R., and B. A. Shearer. 2002. "Extraordinary," "tremendous," "exhilarating," "magnificent": Middle school at-risk students become avid word learners with the vocabulary self-collection strategy (VSS). *Journal of Adolescent and Adult Literacy* 45 (5): 352–63.

Schwartz, R. M. and T. E. Raphael. 1985. Concept of definition: A key to improving students' vocabulary. *The Reading Teacher* 39 (2): 198–205.

Scott, J. 2005. Creating opportunities to acquire new word meanings from text. In *Teaching and learning vocabulary: Bringing research to practice*, ed. E. H. Hiebert and M. L. Kamil, 69–91. Mahwah, NJ: Lawrence Erlbaum.

Scott, J. A., and W. E. Nagy. 2004. Developing word consciousness. In *Vocabulary instruction: Research to practice*, ed. J. F. Baumann and E. J. Kame'enui, 201–17. New York: Guilford.

Sénéchal, M. 1997. The differential effect of storybook reading on preschoolers' acquisition of expressive and receptive vocabulary. *Journal of Child Language* 24 (1): 123–38.

Sénéchal, M., and E. H. Cornell. 1993. Vocabulary acquisition through shared reading experiences. *Reading Research Quarterly* 28 (4): 361–74.

Shaywitz, S. 2003. *Overcoming dyslexia: A new and complete science-based program for reading problems at any level*. New York: Alfred A. Knopf.

Spencer, B. H., and A. M. Guillaume. 2006. Integrating curriculum through the learning cycle: Content-based reading and vocabulary instruction. *The Reading Teacher* 60 (3): 206–19.

Stahl, S. A. 1999. *Vocabulary development*. Cambridge, MA: Brookline.

———. 2005. Four problems with teaching word meanings (and what to do to make vocabulary an integral part of instruction). In *Teaching and learning vocabulary: Bringing research to practice*, ed. E. H. Hiebert and M. L. Kamil, 95–114. Mahwah, NJ: Erlbaum.

Stahl, S. A., and W. Nagy. 2006. *Teaching word meanings*. Mahwah, NJ: Lawrence Erlbaum.

Swain, M. 1993. The output hypothesis: Just speaking and writing aren't enough. *The Canadian Modern Language Review* 50 (1): 158–64.

Tannenbaum, K. R., J. K. Torgesen, and R. K. Wagner. 2006. Relationships between word knowledge and reading comprehension in third-grade children. *Scientific Studies of Reading* 10 (4): 381–98.

Templeton, S. 2004. The vocabulary-spelling connection: Orthographic development and morphological knowledge at the intermediate grades and beyond. In *Vocabulary instruction: Research to practice*, ed. J. F. Baumann and E. J. Kame'enui, 118–38. New York: Guilford Press.

White, T. G., M. F. Graves, and W. H. Slater. 1990. Growth of reading vocabulary in diverse elementary schools: Decoding and word meaning. *Journal of Educational Psychology* 82 (2): 281–90.

White, T. G., J. Sowell, and A. Yanagihara. 1989. Teaching elementary students to use word-part clues. *The Reading Teacher* 42:302–8.

Yopp, H. K., and R. H. Yopp. 2003. Ten important words: Identifying the big ideas in informational text. *Journal of Content Area Reading* 2 (1): 7–13.

———. 2006. *Literature-based reading activities*. 4th ed. Boston: Allyn and Bacon.

———. 2007. Viewing vocabulary: Building word knowledge through informational websites. *ReadWriteThink*. International Reading Association and National Council for Teachers of English. http://www.readwritethink.org/lessons/lesson_view.asp?id=1081

Yopp, R. H. 2007. Word Links: A strategy for developing word knowledge. *Voices from the Middle* 15 (1): 27–33.

Yopp, R. H., and H. K. Yopp. 2000. Sharing informational text with young children. *The Reading Teacher* 53 (5): 410–23.

———. 2004. Preview-Predict-Confirm: Thinking about the language and content of informational text. *The Reading Teacher* 58 (1): 79–83.

———. 2006. Informational texts as read-alouds at school and home. *Journal of Literacy Research* 38 (1): 37–51.

———. 2007. Ten important words plus: A strategy for building word knowledge. *The Reading Teacher* 61 (2): 157–60.

# Appendix B:
# Literature Cited

Achebe, C. 2002. *Things fall apart*. New York: Anchor Books.

Ada, A. F. 1997. *Gathering the Sun: An ABC in Spanish and English*. New York: Lothrop, Lee & Shepard Books.

Arnosky, J. 1999. *All about owls*. New York: Scholastic.

Austin, J. 1983. *Pride and prejudice*. New York: Bantam Classics.

Avi. 1990. *The true confessions of Charlotte Doyle*. New York: Orchard Books.

———. 1991. *Nothing but the truth*. New York: Orchard.

———. 2002. *Crispin: The cross of lead*. New York: Hyperion.

Barrett, J. 1982. *Cloudy with a chance of meatballs*. New York: Aladdin.

Branley, F. M. 1987. *It's raining cats and dogs: All kinds of weather and why we have it*. Boston: Houghton Mifflin.

———. 1999. *Flash, crash, rumble, and roll*. New York: HarperTrophy.

Bruchac, J. 1992. *Thirteen moons on turtle's back: A native american year of moons*. New York: Philomel Books.

Bryan, A. 2003. *Beautiful blackbird*. New York: Atheneum.

Cisneros, S. 1994. *Hairs/pelitos*. New York: Random House.

Curtis, C. P. 1999. *Bud not Buddy*. New York: Delacorte Press.

———. 2001. *The Watsons go to Birmingham—1963*. New York: Laurel Leaf.

———. 2007. *Elijah of Buxton*. New York: Scholastic Press.

Degross, M. 1998. *Donavan's word jar*. New York: Amistad.

dePaola, T. 1978. *Pancakes for breakfast*. Orlando, FL: Voyager.

———. 1984. *The cloud book*. New York: Holiday House.

Farmer, N. 1994. *The ear, the eye, and the arm*. New York, NY: Orchard Books.

———. 1998. *A girl named disaster*. New York: Puffin Books.

———. 2002. *The house of the scorpion*. New York: Atheneum Books for Young Readers.

Forbes, E. 1943. *Johnny Tremain*. Boston: Houghton Mifflin.

Gibbons, G. 1989. *Monarch butterfly*. New York: Holiday House.

Hallinan, P.K. 1977. *That's what a friend is*. Chicago: Children's Press.

Henkes, K. 1996. *Chrysanthemum*. New York: HarperTrophy.

———. 1996. *Lilly's purple plastic purse*. New York: Greenwillow.

Hobbs, W. 1989. *Bearstone*. New York: Atheneum.

———. 1997. *Far north*. New York: Avon.

———. 1998. *Ghost canoe*. New York: Morrow Junior Books.

Howe, D., and J. Howe 1979. *Bunnicula*. New York: Scholastic.

Hunt, I. 1964. *Across five Aprils*. Chicago: Follett Publishing Company.

King, S. 1992. *The dead zone*. New York: Warner Books.

———. 2002. *The shining*. New York: Pocket Books.

Levine, E. 2007. *Henry's freedom box: A true story from the underground railroad*. New York: Scholastic Press.

Mayer, M. 1967. *A boy, a dog, and a frog*. New York: Dial.

McGovern, A. 1986. *Stone soup*. New York: Scholastic.

Myers, W. D. 1988. *Scorpions*. New York: Harper and Row.

———. 1992. *Somewhere in the darkness*. New York: Scholastic.

———. 2000. *Monster*. New York: Scholastic.

O'Dell, N. 1960. *Island of the blue dolphins*. Boston: Houghton Mifflin.

Park, L. S. 1999. *Seesaw girl*. New York: Clarion Books.

———. 2001. *A single shard*. New York: Clarion Books.

———. 2002. *When my name was Keoko*. New York: Clarion Books.

Peet, B. 1977. *Big, bad Bruce*. Boston: Houghton Mifflin.

Prelutsky, J. 1983. *The Random House book of poetry for children*. New York: Random House.

Rathmann, P. 1995. *Officer Buckle and Gloria*. New York: Scholastic.

Rattigan, J. K. 2001. *Dumpling soup*. New York: Little, Brown and Company.

Rawls, W. 1961. *Where the red fern grows*. Garden City, NY: Doubleday.

Rosen, M. 2007. *South and north, east and west*. New York: Walker Books Ltd.

Rylant, C. 1998. *Appalachia: The voices of sleeping birds*. San Diego, CA: Voyager Books.

———. 2004. *Missing May*. New York: Scholastic.

Sendak, M. 1988. *Where the wild things are*. New York: HarperTrophy.

———. 1991. *Chicken soup with rice*. New York: HarperTrophy.

Shelley, M. 2004. *Frankenstein*. New York: Pocket Books.

Silverstein, S. 2004. *Where the sidewalk ends*. New York: HarperCollins.

Soto, G. 1992. *Too many tamales*. New York: Putnam.

Spinelli, J. 1990. *Maniac Magee*. Boston: Little, Brown.

———. 1997. *Wringer*. New York: HarperCollins.

———. 2002. *Stargirl*. New York: Knopf.

———. 2005. *Milkweed*. New York: Laurel-leaf Books.

Steinbeck, J. 1937. *Of mice and men*. New York: Penguin Books.

Uchida, Y. 1991. *The invisible thread: An autobiography in my own words*. Englewood Cliffs, NJ: J. Messner.

Viorst, J. 1987. *Alexander and the terrible, horrible, no good, very bad day*. New York: Aladdin.

Waber, B. 1972. *Ira sleeps over*. Boston: Houghton Mifflin.

White, E. B. 1974. *Stuart little*. New York: HarperTrophy.

———. 2001. *Charlotte's web*. New York: HarperCollins.

Wing, N. 1996. *Jalapeño bagels*. New York: Antheneum Books for Young Readers.

Wood, A. 2004. *The napping house*. San Diego, CA: Harcourt Children's Books.

Zelinsky, P. O. 1986. *Rumpelstiltskin*. New York: Dutton Juvenile.